THE **POWER** OF
EVENTS

Alicia R. Riley

Aster Press
An imprint of Blue Fortune Enterprises, LLC

THE POWER OF EVENTS
Copyright © 2018 by Alicia R. Riley.

For information contact :
Blue Fortune Enterprises, LLC
Cactus Mystery Press
P.O. Box 554
Yorktown, VA 23690
http://blue-fortune.com

Book and Cover design by Kenny Reyes
Cover and Back Photos by Amanda MacDiarmid, Stellar Exposures

ISBN: 978-1-948979-12-2

December 2018

Dedication

The Power of Events is dedicated to future event planning leaders.

I am a true believer in helping people achieve dreams which may not be understood or accepted by others. Regardless of all judgement, persevere and know you have the power to plan life events.

May God continue to bless your talents.

Alicia

This book is also dedicated to my nephew, Ryan. It is because of your true young adult sparkle that I know, I still carry the gift of magic and wonder in my events. With your first limo ride at the age of two and being around private chefs at the age of three, you made me laugh thinking this was a normal lifestyle. When the family is literal and on occasion may not understand our creativity, I watch you continue to dream with your "eyes wide open."

Sonya Askew and Marian Clifton;
The words "Thank You" are not even enough.

Of course, Ronald (father), Barbara (mother), LaTanja (sister), Tim (brother-in-law), Brandon (nephew), Look, I wrote a book. I guess I should have told you guys. Surprise! ummm… love you.

Special thanks to my college sweetheart and husband Kenny Reyes. I dream bigger than most and I know I am dragging you along for the ride. Prayerfully, my endeavors benefit you as well. You are extremely talented and blessed. May God continue to bless your giving heart, playful spirit, skillful hands and courageous mind.

Table of Contents

Foreword

Alicia,

First, I want to thank you for the opportunity to be a part of such a special and momentous occasion! Loved the environment, the elected officials, the ambiance… everything was just perfect. I have performed for more Gala's, Ball's, Fundraiser's, Dance's, etc. than I can even begin to remember and yours was one of the nicest! The decor was exquisite, the directions were clear, the staff were friendly/helpful, the flow was impeccable, and so on. You put on an amazing event and you should feel proud!

Curtis

BrassWind Band

The Planning Journey

I must admit I am writing this book as a person who created her own career. I am not a planner who owns a million-dollar business empire. I am a person who could not pass chemistry to become a doctor and one who failed nursing school twice and could not reapply. My last hope was artistic expression. I have often been complimented on my creativity, and sometimes it seems to be intimidating, to the point that several companies would not risk hiring me for fear I would not conform to their guidelines. Who wants to hire an event planner with an ambition to brand a company as the leading event design/planning agency of the world? My original career goal was to be a doctor, and to this day, I must admit I would like to explore the medical field. However, I knew deep in my heart that becoming a doctor was not my destiny. Even when I was six years old and expressing this ambition, adults questioned my career choice.

"Alicia, what would you like to be when you grow up?"

"A doctor."

"Wow! This little girl has great ambition," people would say, but I might as well have replied that I wanted to be a cow herder. I am sure no one took my answer seriously. As a young person, I knew I wanted to help people, and doctor was the career path to best do so.

In college, I would stand outside my chemistry class, questioning my career endeavors. I didn't know why I was there. Many people aspire to be a doctor or nurse, make it into medical school, pass all the classes and have their career plans work out perfectly. For me, every failing grade was an indicator I needed to reconsider my medical path.

Within my career journey, I had supporters. Trust me, I visited every career counselor in college and, inspired by their guidance, learned to stop dreaming about how I would like to live and started planning my life. But enough of this pity party over my career path. The key word in the preface to my eventual career is "plan." As luck would have it, a serendipitous event soon set me on that professional journey.

During my college extracurricular activities, I stepped up to plan a sorority benefit gala. As part of my responsibility, I researched different decorations that would fit within the theme. My quest ended at a special events prop shop. The store window was decorated like a scene from "The Wizard of Oz." The fairy witch was inside of a huge bubble. It was like looking at the original props from the movie. The owner of the store invited me into the creation room in back of the shop. This is where I saw all the artists making theme décor. From idea to execution, I had no idea people could make money using their imaginations in this craft. At that moment, my mind was made up.

Forget chemistry. I wanted to design.

I was serious about this new career option. I was thrilled to tell my parents I decided to drop out of my pre-med program and become an artist. Okay, that didn't go over well, but I was happy with the direction I chose. Remember the idea that I could have announced being a cow herder? It was pretty obvious "doctor" was not necessarily written on me. Well, maybe someday, but not right now.

The owner of the prop shop mentioned I should meet a local event designer who made a career out of decorating and helping people with their special moments. I kept her name in the back of my mind until I was able to meet her at a bridal fashion show. At the time, my sister was getting married and thought attending the show would give me insight into the event world. I was intrigued by the show, and I knew this designer would be a feature model and exhibit decorator. After the fashion show, the models mingled with the attendees. I spotted the event designer, based on the description from the prop shop owner, an African-American woman with crystal blue eyes. I got up the courage to introduce myself. She welcomed me with a warm smile and a hug. I felt this was a rite of passage as she welcomed me into the field of design.

This impressive and enchanting woman invited me to her home the next day for an afternoon meeting. When I parked in her driveway, I was flabbergasted by the pink brick construction of her home. A welcome flag was swaying against the wind. I swiftly walked to the walnut wood door adorned with a beautiful pane glass design. When I rang the doorbell, it played a Beethoven classic. Answering the door was an assistant with a poodle dog. Oh my! This woman was living in Barbie's dream house, and what blew me away was she was an event designer.

After her assistant greeted me, I looked around the house and saw nothing but beauty. Her assistant walked me into a study with bay windows, wainscoting and double-glass-pane pocket doors. Her study had a custom-built, mahogany desk with matching built-in book cases. The unit commanded the room. Her executive high back, brown leather desk chair was the center of attention.

I thought there was no way she could be an event designer and live like this. Only people from New York and London—not coastal Virginia—have lives this rich.

I kept my composure and accepted an ice water with cucumber from her event assistant. I sat quietly, staring at shelves full of photo albums, guessing which books carried the best photos of her designs. Suddenly, I heard creaks coming from her espresso-colored hardwood floor. I turned around to see an events professional. I stood up and looked directly into her crystal blue eyes, which she mentioned were a unique genetic trait, and I greeted her with a hug. The "star"—which is who she seemed to be to me—held my shoulders and said, "I am here to teach you how to design and would like to hire you as one of my assistant designers." I was speechless and scared. I felt blessed to have such a mentor at the age of 19. This was the lifestyle I wanted. I was on my way.

Later that evening, my heart was full of excitement to tell my parents I was hired to assist an events legend—well, a legend at least for the Hampton Roads, Virginia area. I knew what was going to happen before the conversation took place. I braced for the impact. My parents were not thrilled with the idea and encouraged me to stay focused on studying art, which again, I am sure did not make them happy. I agreed with my parents' strong philosophy about the importance of education, and I did as I was told. I turned down the offer, although I knew I wanted this career and was willing to give it a try. Alternatively, I thought the pre-med department needed to throw me a welcome back party.

I attended a local college in Newport News, Virginia: Christopher Newport University (CNU), or as the locals call it, Harvard by the Bay. In 1996, Christopher Newport, inaugurated a new college president who had a vision of creating an avenue of the arts. This direction was used to connect the college with the local community: new theaters, a football team and a great lawn that would house socials. His vision occurred quickly. As one building was demolished a new state-of-the-art venue was constructed. Little did I know, I would be a part of this phenomenon.

In 1999, I declared my major as Fine Arts Design, with a 1920s weddings concentration. Since CNU did not offer an event design degree program, I had to petition for this major. The college encouraged my freedom and allowed me to write my own syllabus in my design classes. Having a college president who understood how influential events can be helped with my instructors approving my course of study.

Soon after my declaration, I received a letter from the college president inviting me to be a part of his Presidential Leadership Academy. This inaugural program would be the shining light behind CNU. The academy was to encourage perceptive students to attend the university. Several strategies were used to make future students aware of the benefits of this refurbished learning environment: open houses, orientation, formals and grand openings. This would be my first exposure to a plethora of marketing events. I quietly accepted the offer, with the expectation that this opportunity could possibly direct my career journey.

One of many of my job responsibilities was teaching a two-day orientation class in the summer. My first class consisted of 20 freshman students. I wanted to make sure my teaching style was fun and educational. During an ice breaker activity called "tell me about yourself," a student mentioned she was getting married. I quickly told her I would plan her wedding for free. Suddenly my class tutorial became a two-person conversation. I went from peppy game director to a businesswoman. She took me up on my offer, which was shocking, since I had no experience.

My college journey took another shift, from doctor to event designer to event planner. I was clueless about planning anything. I proceeded with writing seventy objectives I thought I would need to learn before executing my first event. I studied napkin folding, table etiquette, how to curl ribbon, constructing timelines, writing memos, negotiating contracts and creating documentation forms. Most importantly, I kept this new adventure a secret from family and close friends. God opened numerous doors for me, and I needed to walk through one of them. I needed to say Yes to my future. I felt confident about my decision. With this information learned, I created a guidebook to special events. Little did I know this guidebook would open the doors to several job opportunities.

I arrived at my first wedding well-prepared. I had a briefcase in my left hand and held my right hand up to God. I was a businesswoman and acted the part. I took full control of the event with confidence. The wedding started on time, and I executed everything according to my timeline and agenda. I received several accolades from the families of the bride and groom.

This one wedding gave me knowledge and confidence to start my first business, Creative Occasions. With my marketing being word of mouth, I contracted with three brides and one graduation party before I graduated from college. On May 14, 2000, at the age of 22, I was charging $75 an hour for my coordinating expertise.

After college, I became a businesswoman with high expectations for events. I was knowledgeable about event design, my first love, and successful at event planning, which was my source of income. I was socializing with the best of the best in the event industry from coastal Virginia. My vendor list increased, as did my client list, with my primary customers from Virginia Beach. I would socialize with business leaders at high-end events, eating calamari, escargot and learning about champagne. I was enjoying this lifestyle. I received an offer for every event planning proposal. I created my destination, my lifestyle and my future. With every job, there is a season, and this was my season. In 2006, I took a full-time job as an event professional to secure a stable income. This is truly where my story begins.

The View from the Chesapeake Bay

In the summer of 2005, I accepted the position of event planner at a beautiful assisted living facility. A majority of the residents had minor mobility restraints or beginning stages of Alzheimer's disease. Their unique abilities did not restrict my creative ambitions. As the new facility's event planner, my job consisted of reading medical records and planning events that related to the residents' lifestyle. Easy, right? Well, I did something different. I read the medical charts in order to plan events that residents had never experienced. These medical records had information about previous lifestyles. Very detailed lifestyles, including their favorite holidays, hobbies, favorite vacation spots and favorite genres of music.

My first event was "A Trip to Jamaica." Coastal Virginia is a military region, so several of the residents had been to Japan, Germany and Hawaii. Why reflect on the residents' previous travel experiences? I wanted to take the residents to a place they had not been. I filled the aquatic center with more than one hundred green and white beach balls. I hired steel drummers and had jerk chicken kabobs served poolside. I had a travel agency place retractable banners in the space advertising Jamaica resorts. The event was the constant topic of conversation at the dining hall later that evening. Residents also sent emails to my supervisor raving about the fantastic experience.

My next event was titled "A Bed and Breakfast Conversation." This was a morning speaker series. My first guest speaker was from the "The Oprah Winfrey Show." I used new bed sheets as tablecloths and placed serving utensils in small pillow cases I made myself. The caterers served French toast, eggs, bacon and fresh squeezed orange juice as the residents embraced the lecture. I was knocking these events out of the park with creativity and originality.

Despite my enthusiastic opinion of my work, however, my supervisor was concerned. I scored an A for creativity and a failing grade for relatability. I had no idea what she was thinking. I was on a roll, and the residents' lifestyles went from ordinary to extraordinary. My last event for the year was a New Year's Eve party. I hired a band with loud drums and placed confetti cannons in the room. Elegant décor filled the space with gold sequin tablecloths. Caterers cooked shrimp tableside with champagne poured on the shrimp, creating a flambé. The louder the drums, the more the residents cheered. There was an extended dinner and dancing all night. At midnight, the startling effects of the confetti cannons made the residents cheer louder. It was a home run event.

My supervisor was even more concerned. She thought I was not reading the medical charts to plan events according to the residents' past. I didn't understand her view. According to my supervisor, I was planning events without an objective. In my eyes, the residents were having fun. My supervisor mentioned this conversation was a warning. Again, not knowing what that meant, I did as told. I read the medical records of several residents, and I denoted commonalities. From this list, I reached out to several companies and requested in-kind donations. My first email was to a local news channel. I contacted the morning news anchors and asked if a few newscasters would sign autographs for the residents. Local hotels agreed to offer culinary demonstrations. A local jewelry bouquet supplied free necklaces and earrings for a makeshift shopping spree for those who wished to participate. Since my supervisor had restricted my decorating budget, I contacted a clown company to teach me how to make balloon arches and columns. On event day, I wore a donated tuxedo, high heels and a fun, messy bun hairstyle.

At 9 a.m., the chime of the elevator echoed down the hallway that connected to the event space. Out came Rip Tide—mascot of the Norfolk Tides minor-league baseball team, three newscasters, hotel culinary troops, local jewelry businesses, community museum operators and a disc jockey dragging speakers and a turntable.

What had I just created?

This was definitely an over-the-top Alicia event, but I had done as I was told. I planned according to the residents' interests: baseball, cooking, shopping, watching the news, going to museums. I just placed it all in one room and gave it a theme name: Valen-Gras Expo (half Valentine's Day and half Mardi Gras).

Testing, one, two… as the disc jockey turned on his personality to hype the crowd, ages sixty-five and up, the residents, nurses and staff were lined up at the event hall thirty minutes before the festivities, a first for assisted living. When the doors opened, the disc jockey welcomed everyone to the expo.

"Welcome to Valen-Gras, a unique event experience," the disc jockey proclaimed in a raspy voice.

Residents gasped with excitement as local newscasters greeted each resident upon entrance. To the residents, they were celebrities. A few women flocked to the cooking area to ask the chef detailed questions about the white wine sauce that was being poured over handmade cheese ravioli. A local hotel gave away free umbrellas. The men laughed at Rip Tide and asked him about the past World Series and upcoming local baseball games. This was a mascot who didn't mind a good conversation.

In the middle of the event, the elevator chimed and out walks my supervisor. She looked around the venue with a serious demeanor.

"Kudos, Alicia," she mumbled, with some hesitation.

Ding. The elevator rang for the third time. Making a grand entrance was the camera crew from the local news station. One of the newscasters stood in front of the camera and began to point out how the community came together to create an everlasting memory for the residents. My event was the feature morning news report. The memorable lesson for me was on the lives of the elderly.

Out of the corner of my eye, my supervisor and I watched nurses and the news crew follow a mute Alzheimer's resident. She picked up a pair of earrings and looked in the mirror. The resident kept saying to herself, "I remember this." In her mind, she was at a real shopping mall.

The nurses, staff and a few residents watched her with amazement as she "shopped." One of the nurses raced out of the venue and went into the medical chart storage. Moments later the nurse returned with her medical chart. The chart indicated when and where she had last spoken. The nurse also located an emergency contact phone number and quickly dialed the resident's daughter, using a medical unit cellular. The nurse placed the "mute" resident on the phone so her daughter could have a conversation with her mom about the event. Tears flowed down the nurse's face as she listened to the daughter on the phone.

All was captured on the morning news report.

We all asked the same question: "Did the event jar her memory?"

At this time, I understood what my supervisor was trying to inform. I am still a believer in vision to revision, but now with an underlying purpose or meaning. I thought I would never be able to work in the medical field due to my inability to pass chemistry, but I learned that day I was the nurse of events or the doctor who performed events. Events are holistic, and they move the mind, body and spirit.

I had been somewhat perplexed about the effects of events. On that day, I knew there was an underlying psychological implication. The event was client-centered, the environment elicited a behavior and there was a response.

My supervisor stressed that events should not be about the glory of a unique centerpiece or a creative idea, nor is it about mass producing, but it is about understanding the driving force behind a person's behavior.

It is no longer about neat designs. It is about designs that matter, a subject that matters and a space that matters. It is planning for the soul, possibly an act of healing.

Think about the daughter who received the phone call where her mother was speaking. Think about the resident who could not communicate but suddenly found her voice because of the event. This is what the power of events is all about.

Valen-Gras was my last event at the retirement center. I resigned to continue to work for myself.

When I left the retirement home, my phone continued to ring from employees asking me to plan weddings, birthday parties and retirement functions. I was back to traveling and spending my days in my element: back-to-back events. Shortly after my resignation, I was hired by a wonderful young couple recommended by the retirement center. I was able to exercise my vision-to-revision technique.

A Bride's Gratitude

The residents and staff at the retirement center continued to support my decision to relaunch my business, Creative Occasions. An employee of the center referred me to a bride who was a health enthusiast, and the groom, a scientist. I accepted the offer to plan their special day. When it came to fluff and wedding day designs, besides serving healthy food, the bride didn't have an opinion. Many times, the planning meetings were canceled because she would rather run and exercise. Besides selecting peach as her wedding color, I did all the design work. The designs were to be revealed on her wedding day.

At the church prior to the ceremony, I was helping the bride with her beautiful wedding gown. After attaching her train, I walked in front of her to give her a smile. I noticed the bride crying a river of tears. She said she couldn't stop crying. She had no idea what it was like to actually be the queen of the ball. The bride was a health guru; yoga pants and tank tops were her specialty. She even made an emergency trip to the tanning salon to hide the tank top imprint, which seemed to be tattooed on her shoulders. Wearing this beautiful gown took her breath away. The bride eagerly walked down the aisle and enjoyed the one-hour ceremony.

The wedding reception was well-decorated. The museum in which the event was held used pictures from her wedding in their publications. I filled the outdoor courtyard with three-foot peach colored lanterns. The guests had peach parasols to block the sun and instead of a cake, apple tarts for this outdoor affair.

The evening went as planned. Moments before her sendoff, complete with sparklers at the end of her reception, she looked at me and said, "I could never truly imagine my wedding day, but it was the most perfect day in my life. Most importantly, you discovered who I was as a person, my dreams and aspirations, and created something that I call 'mine,' my memory, my laughter, and my first moments with my husband."

With my new knowledge, I was taking more time to reflect on the client to design a memorable event. This set me apart from other planners in the area. An event planner is similar to the little Drummer Boy. Playing the drums/planning is my gift, and if I plan an occasion for you, you are receiving my all.

Working steadily as my own boss, I graciously accepted another client's offer to plan a special occasion for my mother, who was turning sixty. I knew a surprise party was in store, and being a professional planner, thought I could design an event that would impact her life. Keep in mind, this was the woman who did not necessarily understand the world of events. The theme I selected for her birthday celebration was Luncheon on the Court, only because the venue was my sister's house, and she happened to live on a court. Ten women were invited to tea, lunch and fun. The concept colors were brown and yellow. I had no particular reason for choosing that color palette, but it seemed right to the occasion. I hired a professional guitarist and piano player. They played the song "Sweet Home Alabama" when my mother arrived because she had been born in a historic town in Alabama. The menu consisted of a full Southern cuisine: honey ham, chicken, mac and cheese, collard greens, green beans and potatoes, lemon pound cake as dessert and sunbathed, sweet iced tea to wash it all down. I also provided personalized to-go boxes for those who could not finish this massive meal. We had party games, including a piñata, as sixty-year-old women beat out their frustrations toward their husbands and children. Great times were had by all.

When my mother arrived, the ten women were

standing outside, sporting beautiful brown parasols with yellow ribbon dangling from the handles. The women were waving to her as my dad dropped her off in front of my sister's house. My mom cried and cried. She cried about the funny memorable moments, and she cried about how this event connected so well with her lifestyle. I think she now understands my profession better and the "power" events have in peoples' lives. The experience was recorded on video.

Two years later, she needed this video to uplift her as she underwent a health scare. Because of the survivor and fighter that she is, she used this event to remember the best times of her life and still better times to come. The photo of her genuine smile on her sixtieth birthday still hangs at the entrance of her home. Ten years later, it's time to plan her seventieth.

Moving Forward

I accepted a job in the summer of 2007 as an event planner for a local college. My realm of events shifted from weddings and retirement home functions to working with dignitaries, celebrities and board members at an educational institution. During my first committee meeting with my colleagues to discuss an awards ceremony, a temp worker mentioned, "No one cares about events. They are never memorable, and events are just a waste of money." I was shocked by her comment. I am sure I had the look on my face of someone telling me the tooth fairy was not real.

I prayed, "God help me teach others the 'Power of Events.' God help me to display peace and confidence so that I may influence the lives of others through my event designs and planning. With every event, help me touch a life. Lastly, I pray for understanding and patience."

Amen.

The Power of Knowledge

The Power of Knowledge

One day, a good friend visited me during working hours. When she saw my business suit, and she looked perplexed. "I thought you would be wearing blue jeans to work as a party planner," she stated. The comment annoyed me and, immediately, I found something that I needed to change. My goal was to prove to more people that event planning is a professional career, and I have changed lives— and the images of companies — through my event planning expertise.

I must prove I have changed an industry with my professional skills.

Welcome to your journey of events. Whether you're a professional event planner, an aspiring event planner, or someone who needs to plan a special day for yourself, you are getting ready to tap into creativity that will impact your life and the people around you. Be thankful you can testify you are an event planner. Shout it from every high mountain, and claim it as a pinnacle of your life's journey.

Whatever your reason for selecting event planning as your field of interest, know you are in for a ride that will transform your values and behavior.

How does one define an "event"? Is it a social gathering? Is it a place where the setting is decorated?

I must say these answers are correct. However, the meaning should not be so literal.

An event is anything that happens in your life. Waking up is an event. Brushing your teeth is an event. Tripping over the newspaper is an event. Take a moment to grasp the concept. These examples are considered life events, and, as a planner, your role is to reveal a new plan based on your previous experiences.

Let's say you attended a Mickey Mouse birthday party. You may have enjoyed this party for several reasons. It was a new environment; the decorations were fascinating; it provided a pleasant social opportunity; you spent time with your friends; it yielded a positive life experience; you had fun. In other words, it was a different experience.

Think of your mind as a filing cabinet. Each file is a situation or occurrence in your life, which constitutes an event. With each new experience, a new file is created. Are Mickey Mouse character birthday parties a new idea? No, but the experience is new. Therefore, it is one to remember. It becomes a new file. Any other similar Mickey Mouse birthday parties will be placed in this file after the first experience. Let's say you attend forty-five Mickey Mouse birthday parties in your lifetime. The "file" will become thick, and some of the papers/memories will become less important. Your first experience become your file starters. Any occasion that is a slight deviation from the normal routine can be a file starter as well. Let's talk about some examples.

FILE STARTER

>> Party 1, Mickey Mouse theme event: Cake, happy birthday song, ice cream, presents

>> Party 2, Mickey Mouse theme event: Cake served by mom, happy birthday song, ice cream, presents

>> Party 3, Mickey Mouse theme event: Cake served by mom, happy birthday song, ice cream, presents

>> Party 4, Mickey Mouse theme event: Cake served by mom, happy birthday song, ice cream, presents

>> Party 5, Mickey Mouse theme event: Mickey Mouse serves cake, happy birthday song played by a live children's band, ice cream sandwiches in the shape of Mickey and Minnie Mouse, present — trip to Disney (new file starter)

Events can have a positive or a negative impact. What if the delivery driver for the birthday cake dropped the cake on the front porch as guests were arriving? This would be considered a file starter as well.

All these files have a mental connection to a person, experience and mood. The files are then connected with a question: What is the importance of this file remaining purposeful and meaningful?

Let's revisit the cake falling on the porch situation.

Person: Cake Driver
Experience: Cake Falling
Mood: Angry

The reason why this file is purposeful: To remember to pick up the cake yourself from the cake shop next year.

All these files are subliminal messages stored in your mind to share with others and to react differently, or the same, if a similar experience occurs.

The first step in planning is interviewing. Remember, an event planner's mission is to change a life experience. The only way to accomplish this is to discover the norm. This applies to a business as well as an individual.

Most planners don't ask the right questions. For example, instead of asking about event colors, ask the client about the colors that brings her or him happiness. The key is to ask open-ended questions and to avoid "yes" or "no" responses.

When working with a business, you may not have the opportunity to interview key operators. Many times, annual reports may offer insight. However, reports normally offer only statistical information and not negative reviews. It may take several conversations and observations to start assembling the personality of the business.

Whether planning for a person or a business, you will ask two types of questions: topical and epi. Topical questions will help you collect information about various principles of discussions. Epi is defined as determining why various principles exist.

Let's start with a personal example: a woman's favorite color may be pink, but the color that brings her happiness is yellow. This is very valuable information for an event planner.

Using epi questions to follow topical questions

is easy. Examine the dialogue below, and notice how each epi question provides an opportunity for the planner to expand his or her knowledge of the client.

> Topical question: What color brings you happiness?
>
> Answer: Yellow.
>
> Epi question: Is there a special meaning with the color yellow?
>
> Answer: It reminds me of the bright days of living in Arizona.
>
> Topical question: When did you live in Arizona?
>
> Answer: I was born there, and I moved away when I was six.
>
> Epi question: What are your favorite childhood memories from the years in Arizona?
>
> Answer: Being around family.

Epi questions allow you to collect detailed information to develop *elements* for planning. Elements are key words from the discussion, such as *yellow*, *bright days*, *family* and *Arizona*.

You will find the initial information clients give you may not necessarily be what their heart desires. Reaching their true desires requires some research that you can conduct with epi questions. You will notice after asking your epi questions, clients will change their thought processes.

Epi questions can be challenging because you know your mission is to slightly open a file that may have been closed for a long period of time. Don't be surprised if tears fall or the client stops to dwell in the moment.

Event planners should conduct client interviews in person if possible. Because you are encouraging someone to speak openly about feelings, an initial interview should be done in a quiet location, and the planner should never hide behind a desk. Make direct eye contact and smile every time you discover an element.

Let's continue the conversation with our Arizona native with some topical questions.

> Topical (on the surface of a new thought): What are your hobbies?
>
> Answer: I think daydreaming is my hobby.
>
> Epi: What do you daydream about?
>
> Answer: About being away from the everyday madness.

Know when to stop asking epi questions and start a new topical question.

You are not a psychologist. You are merely trying to define elements. Responses such as "everyday madness" should not be discovered.

The element from this question is "being away." Now you have elements that will help you build an event: Yellow, bright days, family, Arizona, and being away. These elements aren't related in any way to pink, the client's favorite color.

In a business structure, topical and epi questions are treated the same way. However, in a business, it is important to gather information regarding the overview of the organization. The length of time to get answers to epi questions can extend for several days because of the different personal views and goals of the employees. Each employee provides different missions and viewpoints.

Businesses carry two personalities: one of fact (statistical) and one of truth (a person's actual experience). Think of it as looking at a picture of smiling faces; smiles could mask frustration. Just because they are smiling does not mean that the people are happy. When asking an organizational leader about company issues, the response is usually covered with data, number of products sold, and the total number of employees and, of course, a smile. These facts are important. However, knowing the views of the employees is also important. How do the employees or clientele feel about the progression of the business? These epi questions will begin to bridge the gap between the different possible versions of the event.

I planned a holiday party for a company in which the CEO was the company lead planner. This visionary had a high expectation for the logistical processes, with two bands and three open bars, and a nice end-of-the-year celebration bonus for the employees who attended.

The administrators didn't know until event day, the employees were staging a protest against the management. It was the first time in my career a party ended two hours early because of lack of participation. This event was not money well spent.

Every successful interview includes more than a strong set of discovery questions. Other ingredients are essential for optimal information gathering.

Step One: Client's Disposition

Before you ask the first question, your job is to become acquainted with your client using observation. What is your client's disposition? Is he/she excited, relaxed or uptight? Your mission is to stay neutral during the meet and greet but use the body language as data.

Step Two: Logistics

Be sure to ask about the event date, time, location and estimated attendance. Developing a logistics questionnaire will help you keep your questions organized. It will also prevent the omission of important information.

Step Three: Client's Vision

Every client has a mental picture of his or her event. Ask probing questions about your client's "dream event." After asking a few epi questions, you will probably discover that your client doesn't really have a clear idea of what he or she wants, but this initial data is still valuable. You must know your client's vision before you present a revision of his/her dream event.

After asking a series of discovery questions, examine your data and keep an eye out for the elements.

Step Four: Discovery: Topical and Epi questions

This step takes us back to our important discovery questions. Remember to gather as much detail as possible and use this opportunity to create a composite of your client's, or the business's, personality. This sample conversation includes two elements: sunflowers and bold statements.

Topical: What is your favorite flower?

Answer: Sunflowers.

Epi: Why do sunflowers bring you happiness?

Answer: Because they are bold flowers that are often not used for party decorations.

Step Five: Collect elements or key words that help you create a visual for the event

Let's try another example from a business point of view.

Question: What is the main reason for hosting the event?

Answer: To begin networking with other local businesses.

Epi: Is there a particular business you admire and would like to partner with?

Answer: KLQ industries

Epi: What aspects of that company would you like to incorporate into an event?

Answer: KLQ strong determination and visual advertisements that relate well with the product brand.

The elements would be *determination* and *visual advertisements*.

Step Six: Revision

Using the logistical information, the client's vision and the elements, a planner should be able to produce a sample vision.

Sample visions require practice. The stronger the sample vision, the stronger the planner's creativity.

Have you ever listened to a love song and closed your eyes and could see the lyrics turn into reality? It's like watching a movie in your mind. I call this "the crystal ball of vision" or "sample vision."

> A sample vision is a mental image of the event based on the conversation during a client's interview.

Building an emotional relationship with a client can help in providing empathy toward a person's event. For example, if you have a client who hates the color green, you can compare the client's dislike for green to your dislike for the color red. The more you understand, the more you will display a passion for the event plans. Remember, you are on a mission to create a positive event file.

> *Try This*
>
> Close your eyes, and imagine I placed a rose in your right hand. Can you feel the stem? Can you smell the rose? Does the smell of the rose produce a taste in your mouth, similar to a strawberry? Was there a sound when your hand touched the stem? Does the rose look like a patch of crepe satin? What type of emotion does holding that rose produce for you?

It prompts me to reminisce about the first time I received a rose. If I had a client that mentioned a love for roses, I would think about my rose-related memories to prompt a love for roses that is comparable to my client's love for roses.

15

In the previous chapter, you might have noticed the five senses were used to create a clear picture and emotion concerning the rose. Reality and awareness can be expressed through your five senses, but you can also manipulate your five senses.

Think about a rough piece of sandpaper. What does it remind you of? It reminds me of a tree trunk, so it would be perfect for a forest theme party. Sandpaper place cards can be used to address the roughness of a tree trunk and the relationship a tree has with a forest. You can use a number of objects to define the features you are trying to convey.

On an early morning, I looked outside and found a gloomy sky and trees blowing against the wind. My neighbor picked up her morning newspaper with a sweater wrapped around her arms. What month was it? September? October? No. It was July. But this describes an early fall morning. It is the fall-like conditions that cause us to think about September and October. Our idea of summer weather keeps us from guessing that it was a July morning.

Definitions of objects and subjects can be interchangeable. That is why collecting elements or clue words that produce a vision is important. Taking the elements and placing them in the right context will help the event make sense. Gloomy sky, trees blowing and a sweater definitely do not describe July. However, in some cases, you may not want the elements to make sense.

If I were planning an event representing fall, would I have ninety degree weather with people walking around in swimsuits? Absolutely not. Now what if I was trying to create a new mental file? Would you remember ninety degree weather in the middle of October? Yes. How many planners do you know would dare to take the norm and manipulate it to a point that it would not make sense? Making the unbeliever believe is a big part of event planning. It is also a component of sample vision.

Think about the prior example of the business that

wanted better advertisement to compete with a competitor. What if the networkers entered a room where it was snowing, and, throughout the evening, the winter became spring? With each change of season, letters appeared on the wall. When spring arrived, the word *determination* is spelled across the walls of the room.

To begin the sample vision, gather your elements and create a common theme. These elements must be achievable and tangible.

For example, a client wants to have a Jazz and Blues Fest retirement party for fifty people. According to the client's responses to the epi questions, she remembers dancing to jazz in her living room when she got her first job. Let's use this information to formulate a plan.

Topical: Type of job (fixing computers)
Favorite color: orange
Elements: Dance, jazz, living room, orange

Sample Vision:
Living room: Couches, pillows, old radios, bottled cola, shag rug
Jazz: Instruments, sheet music, records, programs, featured artist, tickets
Dance: Mirror ball, dance floor
Orange: Something edible or visual

Once you have your sample vision, ask yourself, "Am I able to execute this vision?" Once you formulate your sample vision, add your five senses:
Smell: The smell of citrus orange
Taste: Comfort home foods
Touch: Living room furniture
Sight: Couch, pillows, sheet music, room colors
Sound: Jazz music.

Once you reach this milestone, it's time to get creative.

The client's favorite color is orange, so an orange citrus drink could be served. Remember the play on words or the play on your senses. Remember looking out the window and seeing a different picture.

Sample visions are tricky. Remember, just because words are placed in their context with clear definition doesn't mean the definition or context can't change. A breezy, gloomy day with leaves on the ground does not have to signal fall. Sample visions are just an extended thought from your element. They are descriptors. Each thought can be manipulated creatively.

Sample visions may bring fear to many clients because sometimes they don't make sense. It is the fear of rejection. It is the fear of taking a thought and giving it another definition.

What if you had a client who wanted a beach theme? Your element is a beach ball. You told the client that instead of using beach balls as décor, you wanted to use blue marbles. The roundness of the beach ball is represented in the marble shape and the blue swirl is the water. Now what if the marbles were sitting on black sand? Many people would have chosen tan-colored sand because that is what they know. I would select black sand because that is the color I see when I walk on the beach at night. My sample vision is a strong one and would differentiate me from other planners.

Sample visions are what you think of when the elements are introduced, so how would you incorporate the five senses in the marble and black sand arrangement?

The beach carries a smell. Ocean breeze air fresheners or oils could be placed in the sand.

To simulate hearing, I could purchase a digital recorder, record the sound of the ocean and place that recorder on the table.

There are numerous examples of the other senses.

For every task performed during an event, a form should be created. Think of this as a "medical" approach. When a doctor gives you a blood test, he or she uses a blood test form. When you need your eyes checked, the doctor uses a different form. The same should apply for event planners. When you need to order décor, use a décor form, and if you are checking for circuit use, generate a different form. The forms allow you to concentrate on one area. When I am checking for event safety, it is the only item I am concentrating on at that time. I have to make sure I am following the rules and regulations of that area.

Forms are created based on the organization correction needed. For example, what if you are having trouble keeping track of the tablecloth sizes needed per event? In your logistics notes, the size of tables can be determined. As a planner, you need to ask the right questions so you can have the right answers.

After information is gathered, you will begin to create reports that can be presented. An extension of asking topical and epi questions are topical and epi reports. Although topical reports are preferred, epi reports expand on the details of the event. A good planner should write both reports.

A topical report is a one-page basic information sheet. This is not considered a parked report, a completed report specifying all information of the event. The memo begins with a brief explanation of the event objective. Next the logistics are listed, but not in complete sentences. For example, "Event Objective: To build a relationship between the ABC corporation and MJH supply group."

The event mission should also be determined. This mission is a preliminary statement. You should be able to obtain data throughout the event.

For example, "Event mission: To develop ideas that will help with the Jet's merger." At the end of the event, you should be able to answer the question. Were ideas developed to assist with the Jet's merger per this event? What were the ideas? In other words, was the objective met?

Basic logistics: Location, time, date, estimated number of people and cost per person. Although this information could have already been provided to you, always restate it in the beginning of the topical report.

Explaining the budget is very important. If this is a recurring event and you cut costs, you may want to show the comparison. This is optional; however, this should be written in your epi report.

Meal selection is also key. Many corporations believe the type of food being served reflects the health of the company. When asking donors for money, organizations will choose to serve lighter foods as opposed to lobster and prime beef. The heavy meal selection indicates that the company has money to spare.

In an epi report, each aspect of the event is broken down into smaller details.

In preparing epi reports, you are proving that your planning is acceptable based on research. When writing epi reports, keep asking yourself why:

Why did you choose the caterer?
Why is decor not needed for this year's event?
What are your overall recommendations?

As a planner, promote the value of the events by following the rules and processes of forecasting the future. The best way to explain my version of the planning process is with the acronym LOVEE (Logistics, Operations, Vendors, Event and Evaluate).

Logistics is defined as the point of origin.

Who: Who is offering the event? Who is attending the event?

What: What type of event style?

When: What is the date and time?

Where: What is the location of the event?

Why: What is the purpose of the function?

Operations is the core of the business. Who is the manager? What is the budget? What is the event design? What is your event flow?

Vendors: Who received a product bid? Who won the bid? What services are they rendering?

Event: Have the event. Follow your plans.

Evaluate: This can be through surveys or

documenting post-event reports.

Think of the event planning process like a solar system, with the name of the event as the sun. Each *LOVEE* is circulating around every event. Let's take a look at this Event Process checklist:

L (Logistics)

Point of Contact _____

Event Objective _____

___Determine type of event (Luncheon, reception, seminar) _____

___Check calendar for conflicts; this includes city events, holidays and personal conflicts

___Compare last year's date, time and location, if the event is annual

___Determine date and time _____

___Determine location

(List one to three other locations for comparison)

1. _____
2. _____
3. _____

___Reserve venue(s) _____

Guest Lists

___Compare the guest list with last year's attendees

___Develop the guest list in a database

O (Operations)

___Develop a budget

___Timeline

___Agenda

Request Forms and Contracts

___Service request for room set-up

___Reserve parking

___Develop signage

___Obtain permits

__Audiovisual; equipment, city permits

Hotel Services

___Confirm hotel reservations

___Schedule final meeting with hotel

V (Vendors)

Caterers

___Interview three Caterers

1. _____

2. _____

3. _____

___Select Caterer

___Select entertainment and request contract

Invites and Programs

___Determine guests

___Mail letter(s) of invitation

___Finalize design of printed materials (invitations, programs, postcards)

___Finalize guest list

___Mail itinerary to event speakers (if applicable)

E - Event

Confirmation of Event

___Confirm catering order

___Confirm entertainment booking

___Confirm communication plans with staff

Décor

___Table numbers

___Seating charts

___Plan event décor

___Prepare name badges (if needed)

Favors

___Arrange and wrap gifts

___Prepare information packs

Departure items

___Prepare event box with supplies

___Determine event assistant

___Prepare a folder with event documents (maps, phone numbers, seating charts, extra name badges, guest lists)

Event set-up

___Set up venue – place cards, awards, favors, programs

E -**Evaluation**

___Follow up to ascertain if the event purpose was achieved

___Hold a meeting with the event staff to discuss what went well and to determine areas that may need improvement in the future.

A checklist should be like a football play. It should state what should happen, how it should happen, and the time and strategy behind it. A planner should never check and go. Customize each event checklist. What is listed above is a general logistics checklist that could fit the format of most events. However, after planning, you should create a Factoring Checklist.

Event details are connected to the total impact of the experience. A microphone needs batteries and a Wi-Fi connection to operate cordlessly. Let's say your event begins, and the microphone is not even placed on the mic stand. The detail is not the missing microphone. There are two other components missing. In math we learned about breaking numbers down to the simplest form, called factoring. It's the same in event planning. No other details should be remaining. When you add all the pieces back together, it creates the microphone event component.

I once planned an event for two well-known celebrities. It was important that the written programs for this celebrity event carried the correct message to the attendees. With the sellout event, the message of the company needed to be clear. The program would act as the souvenir, and the celebrities were willing to autograph it.

Event Details Factoring

Souvenir book to include:

- Autograph section
- Advertisement space
- Brand message on back of the book

The detail factor should be integrated in the LOVEE Management checklist.

Program Checklist

You are not done with the factoring checklist. You have one more checklist to complete, the program checklist. Of course, a program checklist documents the program itinerary, which can be used as your timeline.

For example, let's think about a wedding:

_____First Dance

_____Cut the Cake

_____Father/Daughter Dance

During a wedding reception, the bride and groom cut the cake. How do you document the checklist?

Cake cutting after first dance (the bride places her right hand over the groom's right hand, the groom will be holding the knife). Documented time: _____.

Never assume the client is aware of the event flow. A planner should have a listing of EVERYTHING and should follow along as if reading a well-written novel.

Now what would you write after the couple feeds each other the cake? Watch them chew the cake and document the time. This may sound funny now. However, you may get a phone call on a Monday morning asking, "Why didn't you tell me to feed the cake to my husband?"

What are you going to tell your bride? "I forgot," or "I thought you knew?" Remember, a planner is the thinking source behind the people who claim the event was all their idea.

All three checklists would be combined for a heavy duty, detailed checklist called Three Forward Operational (TFO), which stands for three checklist systems that document the progress of an event. For example:

June 15, 2015 AR ___Determine type of event (Luncheon, reception, seminar)

12:30 p.m.

___Luncheon__

_____Gold Fork preset _____

Gold Knife preset_____

Purple demi cloth wraps _____

Salad on blue rim plate preset _____

_____Invocation by Pastor John Smith Sitting at Table one_____

_____Salad Catering Manager Sally O. Contact Number greens_____ carrots_____

tomatoes_____

_____Guest at table one does not want carrots _____

_____Place cards on each table _____

12:45 p.m. (contracted time)

_____ Music played by Four Seasons Band POC John McDonald

      (contact number during meal time)

4 Musicians wearing black tux_____

Clarinet _____

Drums_____

Vocals _____

Base _____

The line to the right represents Recipe Check. These items make up for one element. Greens, carrots and tomatoes are components in the salad. You would check these items prior to the event if feasible. The left blank space is for real time when services are rendered. The TFO should match the information on your contracts.

Timelines

A timeline can be infused in the TFO as a program checklist, which is shown in the example above. To write a timeline, you will need to interview the client. This interview process could take hours. During the interview, you are looking for specific instructions. A weak timeline would just state: "first cake, next first dance, and last toast." A strong timeline would ask, "When you walk into the reception room, what would you like to do?" The bride may answer, "I would like to place my bouquet on the head table. Then my wedding court will stand to my right side. I will grab my husband with my right hand, and he will swing me around in a circle. When I stand still, this is the cue to start the 'Love Bird' song. 'Love Bird' will play in its entirety. I will grab my bouquet and stand in front of the head table for a prayer by Pastor Brown, who will be seated at table one. He is the one with the red hair and beauty mark on his left cheek."

Only real times are documented. For example, 12:30 p.m. reception start time is the only non-justifiable time or a time that stems directly from a contract. Planners should never guess on a timeline, unless they are developing place markers.

Place markers are denoted time lapses, or systematic guesses. For example, a singer may be scheduled to perform a song for 2 minutes.

The timeline could read:
6:00 p.m. – 6:02 p.m. Singer

This may not happen, but I have more control over the bride walking down the aisle at 5 p.m., and, according to contract, the caterer should arrive at 5:30 p.m. Remember, you are the lawyer of this event. Don't list guesses on a timeline or a program; list only facts. These times can be shown using different colors on your timeline. All contracted times can be in black, for example, and place markers can be in red.

I planned an event in which the upper management placed markers on the written agenda, which were distributed to guests. A question and answer period was marked from 8:05 - 8:20 p.m. The speaker continued to speak past the written times. How does that make the company appear? The upper management could have written "Q and A following the presentation." It is only acceptable to list when the speaker will begin if he/she is first on the agenda. Never write the time of anything following. This also prevents people looking at their watches. If you felt that you were dragged to an event, how many times would you look at your watch to determine when the event should be over? Place markers are for planners' eyes only.

This is how the timeline and checklist will look with place markers:
Reception begins at 5:30 p.m.

_____(insert real time) Bride places bouquet on the head table (5:31 p.m.)

_____Wedding court will stand to the right side next to the DJ (5:32 p.m.)

_____Bride grabs husband with right hand (5:33 p.m.)

_____Husband swings bride around in a circle (5:33 p.m.)

_____Cue to start the "Love Bird" song. "Love Bird" will play in its entirety. (5:45 p.m.)

_____Bride will grab bouquet and stand in front of the head table for a prayer. (5:47 p.m.)

_____Pastor Brown will be seated at table one, and he is the one with the red hair. (5:50 p.m.)

Once you retype the information, have the client sign the bottom of your checklist, listing a disclaimer that all information is subject to change depending on the event flow. As the planner, you will document times of occurrences. Having a client see your place markers is your preference. I discourage it.

The completed timeline/checklist will look like this:

<u>5:30 p.m. Reception begins</u>

5:32: Bride places bouquet on the head table (5:31 p.m,)

5:34. Wedding court will stand to the right side next to the DJ (5:32 p.m.)

5:38: Bride grabs husband with right hand (5:33 p.m.)

5:38: Husband swings bride around in a circle (5:33 p.m.)

5:42: Cue to start the "Love Bird" song. "Love Bird" will play in its entirety (5:45 p.m.)

5:58: Bride will grab bouquet and stand in front of the head table for a prayer. (5:47 p.m.)

6:00: Pastor Brown will be seated at table one, and he is the one with the red hair. (5:50 p.m.)

6:15 p.m. Food buffet is available to guests

Let's say you asked your neighbor to do a little shopping for you. You presented her a list: Bread, toothpaste and deodorant. You clearly communicated what you wanted, right? Or did you? A list loses its value if all the questions aren't answered.

This is the timeline that is presentable to distribute to vendors and your client:

The Wedding Reception

1:30 p.m.   Videographer arrives at the ceremony location

1:30 p.m.   Photographer start time

2:00 p.m.   Reception Coordinator arrives

3:30 p.m.   Banquet Manager arrives

3:30 -4:00 p.m. Caterer arrives

4:30 p.m.   Disc jockey sound check

5:30 p.m.   Reception begins

6:00 p.m.   Wedding party lines up according to announcing order

6:15 p.m.   Disc Jockey meets the wedding party and pronounces names

6:20 p.m.   Disc Jockey announces that the wedding party will be introduced in ten minutes and guests should locate seats

6:30 p.m.   Introduction of the wedding party

8:45 p.m.   Bar closes

9:15 p.m.   Begin exit line

9:30 p.m.   Disc Jockey's services are complete

9:30-10:30 p.m.   Takedown

** Contact Security if early takedown is necessary

21

Order of Operation

Order of Operation:

- Blessing: guests are asked to be seated
- Bride and Groom are served

Buffet Line Order

- Parents of the Bride
- Parents of the Groom
- Wedding Party and Guests

Toward the End of Dinner

- Toast by the Maid of Honor and Best Man
- Family are welcome to make a speech at this point

Outdoor Celebration

- Bride and Groom leave the room while guests congregate outdoors
- Mother of the bride and bridesmaids are given parasols.
- A semicircle is made around the dance floor by guests

Dancing

- First Dance
- All Couples Dance
- Wait and read the crowd
- Daddy/Daughter Dance
- Mother/Son Dance

Cutting of the Cake

- Bouquet Toss
- Garter Toss
- Last Dance: half of the dance will be the Bride and Groom, and the guests join in toward the end of the song.

Exit Line

- Butterflies handed to the wedding party
- Horns given to the guests
- Flower Girl and Ring Bearer are given two 3' balloons
- Two box dinners should be placed inside the car

Have you ever been at a party where you are standing, or people have to pull chairs and tables from a storage unit? Did the client not submit the right head count or did the facility not place the correct number of tables? Larger events may have designated seating charts for a proper head count. The facility contract or Event Banquet Order may read "10 chairs per table with 30 tables." This is why planners count every chair and table that is placed in the room to confirm seating.

Not only should planners count seating, they should also count everything distributed to guests. For example, I planned a wedding reception where the cake was served only to one half of the room. After this experience I learned to walk around the room and make sure everyone received service.

Another example is when you are serving two meals. This may be hard to keep up with, but who wants a complaining guest because of a wrong meal?

When you document this information, have a form already listed with the total number of tables to be set. Once the information is counted, write in the number of chairs.

Now you can easily do your event calculations: 10 h (Chairs) x 1 T (tables) and 30T x 10h. The "T" is not for the first letter in the word table it is a symbol for a tabletop and the "h" resembles a chair.

This will equal 300 seats, also known as the seats per space (sps). After your calculations, document the time you counted and initial your findings.

Write another list of everything that should be distributed to the guests. Never state the information as "favors" or "a drink." Be specific. Do not simply document the information this way:

Favors, Table One: <u>10</u>

Instead, document the information this way:

Individual bubbles, wrapped in tulle with pink bow, Table Two <u>10 pps</u> (per place setting)

Table Three <u>10 pps</u>

Table Four <u>10 pps</u>

Whether working for yourself or with a company, you are responsible for creating or learning an event management system. Many corporate event-planning jobs will require experience in this area before consideration of hiring. With all the information you will be collecting, there must be a way that it can be easily stored and processed for future use.

To begin, each event should be assigned an event category and code. For example, a holiday party could be assigned "Social HP-1809." The category is social. *HP* stands for "holiday party" and 1809 is the year and month of the event; however, the year is dated first, with the month listed second. On a computer database, you should be able to identify this event several ways. Just typing "HP" should pull all the holiday parties that your company has hosted. Typing "18" should showcase all the events that occurred in 2018.

There are several different uses for an electronic management system. This could include contact information and connections to social media and project management reports. When you first hear about an event, document the name of the event and that it is in pending status. Once an event is approved, change "pending" to "active." Let's say your supervisor would like a list of all the events you are working on. This will make for a great spreadsheet. When the pending event becomes active, document the start date. Document the event date and document the file completion date, this is not always the date of the event. In many cases, you will send out thank you notes and surveys. You may need time to verify head count.

Active File: Start date June 5, 2020
Event Date: August 16, 2020
File Completion Date: December 12, 2020

Once the file is complete, document it as a parked file. This event took eighteen months to complete. If the event is annual, it will immediately go from "parked" to "pending" status as you start planning for next year.

The parked file should contain the following: checklists, agenda, budget, survey and attendance count.

I can also print parked reports that include the menus that I served in previous years. Sometimes parked reports can help when I am planning an event that is similar to a previously planned event. These reports also help with invitee counts or indicate flaws that needed to be corrected.

Consider generating a management file for new events upon your first notification. When I attend a meeting, I may bring reports of previous, similar events. The files mention the stats, ideas and after reports from the previous three years and the after report. Now, just because this is often the process for businesses, you can also create a filing system for your own dinner party or birthday parties. These files are great keepsakes. Imagine if your parents documented the cost of your first birthday party: What went right and what could have been corrected for year two festivities.

For example, I once went to a backyard BBQ where several tents were placed randomly around the facility for shade. The anchor that attached the tent to the ground was black. As the evening went on, people could no longer see the cord, creating a safety hazard. Several people tripped over the cord. What if this event was annual and, for the next six years, this backyard BBQ host created the same safety hazard? Sub reports could prevent this from happening again.

_____ All electrical plugs have been checked
Time Performed_____ Initial _____

_____ Candles are not near any debris
Time Performed_____ Initial _____

_____ Sound Check (hearing hazard)
Time Performed_____ Initial _____

_____ Tents secured with proper weights –
Wind factors
Time Performed _____ Initial _____

25

I use "information at a glance" to begin and end my event files. Many times, organizations will have brief questions about events. This is an easy tool to use that is geared for supervisors to carry to meetings or to just refresh everyone's memory on the purpose or goal for an event.

Name of the event
Date of the event for the past three years (if this is an annual event)
Chair of the event and supervisor of the event (Different supervisors mean different opinions. Many times there is a person who approves an event.)
Location: name and city of the venue
Budget: The total amount that was allotted, and the amount spent.

Throughout the duration of the event, you will see the overall budget increase or decrease. It is a good idea to keep track. Who did you make payments to and why? This is a good time to spell out the reasons why you purchased items.

Butterflies and Bubbles Birthday Bash

Will Hawkins Photography

Chef Johnna Hamlin, Impressional Sweets
Keith Cephus Photography

A Bride's Gratitude

"I could never truly imagine my wedding day,
but it was the most perfect day in my life."

Cocktail Table Front Arrangement with Swooping Table Cape
Model: Amanda MacDiarmid
Nadere's Photography

Illusions Holiday Party
Nadere's Photography

White Glove Festive Service
Nadere's Photography

Bubble Gum Machine Table with Gumball Colored Macaroon Treats
Melon Ball Sparkling Cider and Lemon Tarts
Chef Johnna Hamlin, Impressional Sweets
Nadere's Photography

Shrimp Taco with 24 Karat Gold Garnish
Chef Johnna Hamlin, Impressional Sweets
Nadere's Photography

Fire and Ice Dinner Party
Nadere's Photography

Orchid Chandelier Suspended from a Cloud Box
Amanda MacDiarmid, Stellar Exposures Photography

Treasure of Flowers
Amanda MacDiarmid, Stellar Exposures Photography

Experimental Educational Elastic (EEE) Décor
Summer Soirée Outdoor Scape
Kenny Reyes, Photographer

Outdoor Tablescape
Nadere's Photography

Sparkles Luncheon
Nadere's Photography

Cold Pyro Fill the Air at the Sparkles Luncheon
Nadere's Photography

Unique Elegance
Chef NaKeisha Cummings, Pink Flames Catering
Nadere's Photography

Venue versus Space

In decorating, it is important to visit the venue, the location in which the event will be held. Venue can be a hotel or a garden clubhouse. At the venue, you will examine the space. *Space* is defined as "the actual room in which the event will be occurring." When entering the space, you will collect Space Renovation Data (SRD).

The ceiling height can be determined by your height. You should know your height with your arm reaching above your head. If you stand on a six-foot ladder, would you be able to touch the ceiling? With one glance, you should have an estimate of the ceiling height. Always confirm your guess with the actual measurements of the room. Pay attention to ceiling construction. For example, many hotels have ceiling tiles. The tiles are connected by a metal grid. Therefore, you can rig a ceiling using magnets.

Look at the floor. Is there a particular color scheme in the floor pattern? See if the carpeting is worn. If the carpet is worn, you may not want to have the décor from the ground up. You may consider midway décor or ceiling to midway.

What color are the walls? Because there are several shades of white, you may want to document the color of white it reminds you of (yellowish white, ivory or vanilla cream).

Room lighting is very important. Play with the dimmer switch. What lighting gives the best glow?

Purchase a laser measurement tool with various applications to include area, volume and exterior. These measurements can be transferred to a computer that can illustrate the venue.

There are several ways to set a room, with each setup having its own room calculations based upon the square footage. A banquet room that will have 72" tables carries this calculation:

Number of people x 12.03 = the square feet needed to hold the total amount of guests

Cocktail reception: 9.47 x the number of attendees = space or the square footage needed

Theater style: 9.00 x the number of attendees = space

Venue checklist

The purpose of the checklist is to create a proposal that gives the best argument for the venue selected.

Name of the venue

How is the venue most often used (meetings, weddings, conferences?)

Location

Room capacity per setup option (theater, banquet, classroom)

Caterers (Exclusive caterers?)

Tables, linens, chairs (What is the quality of the items? Are the chairs stained? What is the quality of the linens?)

What menu is being recommended for the time of year? (Some venues offer holiday packages)

Bartender charges

Minimum food and beverage cost

How early can your caterer arrive the day of the event?

Are any fees negotiable?

How early can you set up the event?

Is there a discount for paying early?

Can the room rental fee be waived?

Location of the bathrooms

How clean are the bathrooms?

Is the parking lot close to the venue and the event space?

Will an event tech cost extra?

Does the venue have internet access?

Describe the entrance of the event

What is the wallcovering?

Is there an entrance to the venue in front of the event space?

What other events are going on during your event?

What decor is not allowed?

What other organizations have used this event space?

Ask for a list of references and document the feedback

Does your sample vision fit your space?

Where is the loading dock?

It is important to know any environment can be manipulated. If the walls are grayish white, it may affect the presentation of the food, and if you are working with a bride who is wearing white, off-white may dull the color of her dress. If wall color needs to be changed, consider having a pipe and drape system for the walls. What about using up lights? This may help in adding color to the space.

How do you know if the room is too spacious? The best way to determine is by the yawn and stretch technique. In a space, your fingertips should be touching another person. Many people prefer to have more space than needed. To determine this, use epi questions. Ask your client if he or she wants to feel embraced by all the family and friends. I call this the claustrophobic event. Claustrophobic events are wonderful for baby showers or eightieth birthday parties. You want to feel the support. However, if crowds make your client nervous, allowing more space than needed will help the person relax.

Environmental Changes

The definition of décor is changing of the environment. The environment can change with anything from the smallest detail to gutting the room and replacing all fixtures and carpeting. If the room maintains a cold temperature, you may adjust the thermostat. This is an example of environmental change.

It is a planner's responsibility to transform the event space. Consider these questions: if guests wear all white clothing, would this be considered an environmental change? If I am listening to classical music, and I change the music selection to country, is this a change in the environment? The next time a client tells you that décor is not desirable or affordable, educate him or her on what décor is. Decor includes audio, human, light and more. Just getting your close friends in one room will change the décor.

For example, to enhance a beachscape, guests could be encouraged to wear sundresses and shorts. I would place electric fans to resemble a summer breeze from the ocean. The lights could be dim to reflect a sunset.

Decor Research

Becoming a planner takes more than just knowledge of the right party store. After asking the right questions, you must know how to use the information. A planner's ability to produce incredible work is based on two elements: fear and knowledge. People do only what they feel comfortable doing; therefore, the greater the knowledge, the greater the opportunity.

Obtaining knowledge to lessen the fear is done through research. A great planner should know every aspect of an event. From how to fold the proper napkin to how to operate uplights, it is important that you are the main information center for your client. You are the expert, so you should know that colors and designs will change the presentation of the food. You should know the latest designs, famous designers and premium flowers.

Several of my event planning colleagues gather to discuss trends and design possibilities. This collaboration helps with developing ideas and offers a discussion on how to utilize the growing event supplies market. Not knowing how to create an event décor scheme is not an option. As I mentioned before, having all the education and certification does not guarantee planner nor decorator status.

Let's say I wanted to have a chocolate party. I want my centerpieces to be fake chocolates. How do I make that happen? Many people would use paper cutouts or real products concealed with bug spray, but what about taking a brown crayon and placing it in the microwave until it melts? Crayons are wax. Once you have liquid wax, pour the wax in a chocolate mold and there you have it: fake chocolate. Creativity is all about knowing how to manipulate a product through the knowledge that you carry.

How do you start to research? First, develop a list of everything you think you would need to know to be a decorator/planner. For example, a good planner would need to identify flowers, wines and proper table settings. The planner also needs to explore the use of ribbon and learn the proper way to fold napkins. Your goal is to have more than seventy-five items on that list. Once you have developed this working list, begin your research. Your goal is hands-on first; many cities offer parks and recreation classes that may help you with getting hands-on experience. Next, try videos and the internet. When you use the internet, find sites that will allow you to follow along with the instructor.

Volunteer if you are a member of an organization, church or if you know of someone having a party. Occasionally, I host dinner parties at my home. This gives me experience on a smaller scale. My husband has been my biggest guinea pig. Date nights became event practice nights. I have devoted many date nights to learning how to pair wines, create proper centerpieces, menu cards, place cards and more. Practice, practice, practice.

Next, learn to think outside the box. The best place to learn is at a museum. Look at a painting, develop/analyze emotions and write down how you would make this image in an enclosed space. If the picture looks cold and gloomy, how would you change the event environment to be cold and gloomy? Write down all the key elements in the picture and develop a centerpiece. With the title of the art piece being the event theme, challenge yourself.

Buy one flower every two weeks and ask the florist the name of the flower and the best way to keep the flower alive.

Buy two LED lights and change the lighting atmosphere even in a small environment such as your home.

Trick of the Trade in Event Design:
The Childhood Secret

A little trade secret about planning is the five percent rule. Five percent of the details of your event should be childish. This can be addressed in any fashion. For example, if you are setting up for a board meeting with notebook paper, bottled water and pens, the pens could be a mix of colors, like a box of blue, yellow and red crayons. You will see people look at the pen set, knowing that it reminds them of childhood. The clients won't mention it, but for a brief second, they will have a flashback.

Once I planned a very elegant gala. This black-tie event consisted of mayors, congressional representatives and CEOs. The night was filled with guest speakers and a plated dinner. In the middle of the evening, the guests were invited to a dessert extravaganza in a separate party room filled with misted fog, bright lights and flambé stations. The guests' eyes lit up, and even the host called it the highlight of the night. The elements representing childhood were the bright colors of the lights and the sweet desserts. Big pieces of sloppy chocolate cake served with ice cream and sprinkles will excite anyone.

Don't Become a Convenience Store Decorator

Back in the 1990s, I remember going to a local Hallmark store and seeing a prepackaged party kit. The kit consisted of eight cups, 16 napkins, eight plates, one tablecloth, eight blowouts and one party sign. Now there are stores that make party decorating easy and simple. In one 30-minute trip to a party store, I can get everything I need but the cake.

I have seen many inexperienced planners use these party stores as their main source for party supplies. If you plan to ask epi questions, plan to change your shopping locations. It is important to know *how* to use a party planning store.

Sometimes you want your events to be whimsical. For example, if I wanted to have an informal tea, I might go to the party store and buy paper cocktail napkins. It is important that the convenient store doesn't become your go-to outlet. I prefer to use party stores for adding details — a pack of cocktail napkins or little umbrellas to go in a mixed drink. How would you feel if you witnessed a person rummaging throughout a party store while wearing a t-shirt that read *Professional Event Planner*? I would be curious about the additional enhancements that would be detailed at the event.

At the other extreme is badly-made décor. A former client mentioned she was in need of a planner and not an event decorator. The client mentioned she had a "fabulous wedding decorator," but did not mind me attending a decorating meeting to offer any advice or suggestions. When I arrived at the meeting, I saw a sample of the centerpieces. The centerpiece was a canned food container wrapped in fabric with a candle sitting on top and a peacock feather hot glued to the pillar candle. Next to the wrapped canned food container were silk flowers that were falling apart. This bride was very dear to me, so I listened to the designer and left the meeting. Later that night, I called the client and questioned her design vision. It was clear the event designer created this convenient-store décor based on her limited decorating knowledge. Anybody can claim to be a decorator, and after the conversation I had with my client, the decorations changed for the better. The moral of this story is a convenient store planner is anyone who does not carry knowledge on purchasing party supplies. A perfect event planner should carry knowledge on where to go and whom to ask to develop any event scheme. Think of all the elements that will be collected in one event counseling session. What if you had no idea how to make the sample vision a reality? Your creditability for event designs could be diminished.

With every event, a budget is associated. A good planner understands money is limited at every event. A budget is given to you for a reason, and that is to limit your spending while mastering a spectacular event. I often look at budgets as my own checking account. If I had to trust people with my money, I would not want them to overspend. I often have to ask the client what part of the event is most important. Many people may say food or décor. This gives me a guideline on where I can cut expenses. If food is important, then I can limit the total cost on favors.

Budget Line Item

Factoring checklists are used to identify elements of a product. From the factoring checklist, you can generate a focus sheet. A focus sheet identifies fine costs: items that may cost a couple of cents but add up to the total budget.

For example, hanging tulle is more than the cost of tulle. With the tulle material comes tape adhesive, curling ribbon and a ladder. So $1 per yard is now $1.50 per yard for the extra materials. Subtract Budget $ from Actual $. Place the remaining cost, to the next budget line item.

Tulle Ceiling Drape

Expense: <u>Pink Tulle, 10 yards</u> Budget: <u>$100</u> Actual: <u>$59.58</u> = <u>$40.42</u>

Expense: <u>Tape</u> Budget: <u>$40.42</u> Actual: <u>$3.89</u> = <u>$36.53</u>

Expense: <u>Fishing wire</u> Budget: <u>$36.53</u> Actual: <u>$2.00</u> = <u>$34.53</u>

Expense _____

Budget $ _____ Actual $ _____ = _____

Expense _____

Budget $ _____ Actual $ _____ = _____

Budget: $100
Actual (add all actual costs): $65.47
Net: Budget $100 – Actual $65.47 = Net $34.53
Don't forget to add your cost per hour for labor.

Budget Time

A rule most planners do not follow is keeping account of time. It may take one hour of travel to buy the product and two hours to display the item. Now your tulle drape costs $70 because of the other factors. Do not forget that time equals cost.

ALL CENTS SHOULD
MAKE PERFECT SENSE!

Budgeting is a thinking style. Your event should have a sense of purpose. You are not in competition with yourself trying to spend a certain amount of money. Making sure that each expense is appropriate to the occasion is essential. Once, I worked at an event planning corporation where employees would buy birthday gifts out of the corporate budget. Once the employees got caught and had to explain to management why lingerie was bought for an event, the corporation put a process in place that I still use to this day.

Spending Why?
Why Tulle?
Why the food selection?
The process started with requiring each employee to use preferred vendors. These vendors sold only items that were event oriented. If an outside vendor needed to be used, the employee would have to write

a memo on why this vendor was chosen. Next was the approval of the quotes. Each employee needed to show that vendors were researched. Last was the approval of another event planner or someone else who could support every decision. This approval process is not to stop your creativity or to tell you not to use the vendor you chose, but to offer suggestions.

I was asked to review the work of an event planner who was trying to purchase wine for an event. When I read over her event report, I saw that she was planning to buy the wine from a local grocery store. I suggested buying from a local winery. Not only could the winery be mentioned in programming, but the local winery also gave a tremendous discount just for the recognition.

Exercise your budget with small items. For example, I host a tailgate party every year. I am given $2,000 to make a big impact on the corporation, and every year, I spend $300 of the total allotted amount. It is important to change the language of finances. Finance means getting the most for your money, which reflects the purpose of the event. With $300, I was able to purchase food, décor, entertainment and door prizes. I must stay focused on the mission of the event and make sure the participants are happy. It does not take much to change an event. Again, success is all about the resources.

Your Service

Every coordinator must be aware of the false checkbook client, a person who claims money is low. The small violins start playing, and the client begins to weep. Then you feel bad, and you give a cut on the cost. Then you start to realize that your client spent $10,000 on a photographer and $5,000 on special gobos, and you feel cheated that you only charged the client $300 for your services — a $600 cut from your normal rate. I learned if the client knows you offer quality services, he or she will pay for that quality. I have been caught in this triangle several times. I work harder, and I sweep up the client's tears, only to see the client spend money on everything but me.

Perceived Value

I was in the midst of planning a holiday party for which I stayed under budget. The theme was winter based. I offered hot chocolate to keep with the winter theme and horse and carriage rides before the event. I was very nervous about hosting part of the event outside. The event venue was for a state-owned corporation. The governor announced weeks prior the state was in financial default and budget cuts were coming down the pipe. Showing a horse and carriage on a state property could lead to an image of abuse of funds. I removed the outside activities. What I needed to understand was perceived value or the cost people place on your event by viewing or by the importance of the product.

Perceived value can also be positive. Budget brides often buy carnations or Baby's Breath without knowing that the value of these flowers is considered lower end. However, a bride can invest in two calla lilies, oversized leaves, and get a better perceived value.

29 Vendor Reports

Vendor Coordination Reports (VCR) are needed for every event. As much as I would love to be the caterer, florist, decorator, musician and ice artist, it is nearly impossible for me to perform all these tasks. Once you have an idea, you will most likely contact a vendor who will bring it to fruition. Vendor reports help you make sure your idea is tracked. Unfortunately, your creative juices may end up the property of the vendor if you are not careful.

A vendor report must state the name of the company and a list of everyone handling your file. The report will list all dates and times at which services should be rendered. Leave a space on the vendor form for time and duty comparisons. For example, if you have a vendor state on a contract that the arrival time was 5:00 p.m., and the vendor showed at 5:20 p.m. make sure that this does not affect the event as a whole.

Let's say a DJ carries a song list, and his vendor report states that certain songs should be played. Use the report to document the missing songs and report it to the DJ. These reports will help you stay on top of the game.

When a vendor enters a party space, ask for a business card and staple it to the vendor report. In some cases, you may never meet the vendor prior to the event date. I worked with a photography company that decided to switch representatives the day of the event. When I asked for a business card, I noticed that the details did not match the contract.

It is important that the right vendors are in the right location. Many banquet halls will have several setups in one day. I have experienced one vendor set up a wedding cake in the wrong section of the room. Imagine a bride walking into a room with two wedding cakes present or the bride who has a cake missing.

Safety checks for vendors are important. Many vendors may need outlets or wiring to make an event happen. You are making sure that your guests are safe by making sure all plugs are taped to the ground. You are also responsible for not blowing a fuse in the middle of an event. Part of safety is knowing the amount of amperage being used.

Vendor Coordination Report

Contractor's Name:
Company:
Time of Arrival:
Contracted Time of Arrival:
Time of Completion:
Est (Estimated set time):
Business Card:

Description of Work:
Any Faults:

Safety Check:

Three categories make up an After Report: Event Improvements, Event Recommendations and Event Success.

The Event Improvements section should be written first. These are items that you forgot to take care of during the event. I once forgot to check the meal for proper selection. Those sitting at the head table notified me that what they ordered was not what was being served. Why didn't I catch that? I should have noticed that beef and chicken don't look alike.

Event Recommendations can be for your vendors and yourself. I noticed at an event that the buffet line was dirty. After politely asking the waitstaff to keep the line clean, I wrote a recommendation letter to the company and noted the recommendation in my after report.

Event success gives you a pat on the back. If you caught the meal that was served incorrectly before the second person was served, pat yourself on the back for having a good eye. Event success is also listening to the comments of other people. Noting that the chicken had good flavor and the table number that the comment came from will make your host feel good.

The last form is reserved for proving cases. I once did an event where I was told I did not have the correct number of seats. Now, I knew the head count. Plus, I did my count form. At the event, I went to the highest spot of the arena and took a picture of everyone standing next to their seats. Following the event, I was prepared for a day of madness and being blamed. During an aftermath meeting, I took out the pictures of the seating area, showing twenty empty seats in the middle row. The number of seats was correct.

After creating all these forms, you have options of what to do with them. If a client says that the event was a success, lock the forms in a treasure chest and throw away the key. Never show the client. The forms help you pay attention to detail. If you have a complainer on your hands who claims you did everything incorrectly, show your client the book and remind him or her of everything that did go well. Sometimes, clients will forget something occurred.

One mistake planners make is not reading contracts or not knowing how to interpret them. When a contract is given to me, I highlight the information with specifies needs, costs and services. Then I generate a list of all the needs of the client. When a contract is returned to the vendor, attach a memo contract restating the terms listed and your expectations of the vendor. Contracts are meant to protect the vendor first. Make sure the vendor understands you have needs as well.

Memorandum

To: Owner of Bell Florist
CC: Bride
From: Special Events Coordinator
Date: September 9, 20XX
Re: Wedding Flowers

Per your contract delivered on September 5, 20XX, all flowers should be delivered to the Host Hotel. When comparing the notes taken during the consultation prior to the contract rendered, a need of hydrangea in each bouquet is highly important because it holds a special meaning for the bride. Per our first visit, I requested a written outline of all the flowers, which I received on September 1, 20XX. It is expected that all flowers listed per that document be placed in each bouquet as well. I understand that major adjustments to floral designs cannot be made after October 7, 20XX. Therefore, a follow up-meeting will be scheduled before the deadline. If any changes need to be made in flower selection due to delivery or product issues, a courtesy phone call or email is expected.

As an event planner, my number one goal is to make sure my bride and groom are happy and feel comfortable with the vendors that they selected. This memo is to stress the importance of making that happen. On October 16, 20XX, my duties as the wedding planner will cease. Therefore, any further discussion of the wedding flowers must be addressed directly with the bride and groom after this date.

The week before the event, I issue another memo that restates the expectations of the vendor, the timeline and contact information. Vendors know I take my events seriously. In my years of experience, I have seen several vendors fail to work according to their contracts. On the other hand, many vendors appreciate the updates and memos.

I went to a motivational seminar that was advertised widely within my community. When I arrived, I saw a stage sitting in the middle of the arena. Surrounding the stage were nice mum plants. I was prepared to hear the speaker and get motivated by words of wisdom. The host of the event came out with cue cards and started to read a two-sentence bio about the well-known speaker. Then the lights went dim. I was ready to enjoy the show. Then, suddenly, fog came out of nowhere, fireworks shot in the air, and streamers went shooting across the room. The lights started to spin, and confetti was dropped. People started to toss beach balls, and suddenly the speaker appeared. Wow! What an unusual entrance for a person who is not God! With all this fanfare, I was guessing the show would still be good. It wasn't! The speaker put me to sleep within the first word of welcome. What was this all about? What a waste of money.

The next person who came up to speak was a no-namer. This guy had the same fanfare, but, this time, brought a totally different message. His message spoke directly to me and made me reflect on my life, and to top it off, his sense of humor just stole the show. I wanted to hear more about the way he lived. The speaker even mentioned how crazy the seminar was and that the programs and fanfare were dumb.

I am sure the explosion and confetti were meant to brand the event as the biggest item that ever hit that arena. However, the program director should have made sure that the special effects did not hurt the dynamics of the event.

Let's talk a little about special effects. *Special effects* is another name for "danger" and "caution." Some special effects, such as fireworks and flash pots, require permits. Many times you need to check with your city guidelines to make sure you are following the proper protocol.

At the seminar, the event planners thought it was a great idea to shoot streamers in the middle of the motivation program. Well, the streamer cannon went off before intermission. During intermission, I watched streamers get wrapped in women's high heels. One woman became so upset with the amount of trash on the floor and the people getting hurt that she complained to the arena workers that the streamers should be picked up at once.

I like streamer special effects because of the easy clean up. They usually get shot in one area and can all be picked up in one sweep of the hand. As a planner, you must plan for the streamers to be picked up. Having them placed on the floor may look nice, but may not be in the best interest for the event.

Confetti cannons and mines are great if you want people to get startled. Confetti is the least of my favorites because of the mess it produces. Some confetti is flammable! When I do weddings, I still make sure no candles have flames when cannons are being fired. If you do not like the noise, you can get a confetti blower. This is great for New Year's Eve parties. The confetti now are made out of products that biodegrade with water. The event planner can spray the area with water if possible to remove the confetti. It makes for a very easy cleanup.

Smoke and fog are great as well. Many times, throughout a dinner party, before I call guests in to be seated, I will drop a piece of dry ice in a flower arrangement. As the guests are seated, fog fills the table while I serve sorbet to cleanse their palette. Now, some fog machines produce an odor. Many people with lung concerns have a difficult time handling the fog in a tight space. Again, there are dry ice machines that do not offer the smell.

I offer you this challenge to create your own special effect. It could be everyone using a cellphone flashlight at the same time. Maybe host a fall dinner party and have leaves drop from the ceiling during dessert time. I encourage everyone to be an innovator. I did an event where twenty battery-operated butterflies filled a garden party during tea time. Some butterflies sat on the shoulders of the guests, and many sat on the handles of the teapots. The women loved it. I must admit several people were startled by the flying bugs, but after about five minutes, everyone enjoyed their beauty.

Sometimes, events are three-ring-circuses. You place all this fluff to get nothing in return, or you include all this fluff, and you get something in return that has nothing to do with the fluff. I have mentioned several times in this book that great events touch on the five senses, but what if the five senses are abused? Can such a thing happen? A circus is made up of three rings, flashing lights and loud noises. These distractions make you think more is best when, in reality, the clown is just doing three cartwheels in a row. Wow! How amazing! Three whole cartwheels! What would be like it you took away two of the rings, the lights, and the fireworks and the clown took off the makeup before doing the cartwheels? What changed? In my eyes, you are able to see the true person with his or her talents and abilities. What if you placed a singer in the middle of the stage and removed the audience, band, speakers and microphone, and then sat in the last seat in the back of the room? Finally, you cued the singer to sing one of your favorite songs. Because you are sitting in the last row, the singer has to use every breath, every note and every part of her soul to enable you to hear it. How would you feel sitting in this room? In my case, every hair would be standing up on my arm. I would thank God for being a part of such an experience.

What I am getting at is don't overlook the reason for the event. Many times, I am hired just for the logistics, and I have no idea what the program is. Or I will plan the logistics first and ask the reason for the event later. This can't happen. The program is the icing on the cake.

Let's say you were planning a seminar with a guest speaker. In the seminar scenario, the program is the speaker and not the branding of the event. Now let's use some event planning experience to change the guest speaker. What if the lights went dim, and the only thing you heard were the voices of empowerment? Then the music came up and people started to clap. Then after the speech, you got all the information about how you can help yourself. Then the confetti dropped, and the fireworks erupted. Now you are on a high because it was grand fanfare for a motivational speaker, the focus of the event.

When you plan an event, what is the focus?

My sister was a school teacher for a short amount of time, and the best assignment, in my opinion, was if you could invite any five celebrities to your house for dinner, who would they be? What would be your focus of conversation?

My focus is to hear them elaborate on their success and wisdom. Now you know this is a dinner, so you will have to balance a meal, décor and entertainment when, really, the only thing you want to do is to hear their profound words. The solution is to keep everything low. Serve light foods that don't require a lot of chewing, and time when people would have their mouths closed. The flowers on the table may be natural so no one pays attention to them. The focus is about the time spent and all the memories that you would get from the experience. Now on Monday morning, what would your coworkers ask you? Yes, they will ask what was served. Next questions: "What did they talk about?" "How did the celebrities look?" "Did they bring their spouses?"

Let me ask you this question: If a celebrity was coming to your house, how long would it take you to prepare? In my case, between cleaning and mending couches and preparing a menu and testing the menu, it would take months. So don't think just because your event is program-oriented that you don't have to do as much work because it is still an event.

Have you ever thought about being a program coordinator? This person does not handle the logistics of the event, but makes sure that the main focus of the event is understood. Maybe this person helps with printable programs and layouts of the program. Why should this person speak first over another? I am sure you know that everything is a strategy.

In a program, the purpose of the event is stated. This is usually done with an announcement. "Welcome to greatest show," or "Let's welcome Mr. ___" just restates the reason why attendees are participating. Many programs work on a bell curve, where the bottom is just a build for what is left to come. The middle is the best and the ending puts the event to rest. Often planners place the best at the end, which will leave the viewer asking for more. In a program, you have one opportunity to make an impression. Offer excitement and prominent information in the beginning, in the middle and in the end.

The programs that disappoint me are the ones where people read verbatim from a book or script. It is important for the speaker to prove his or her own story by using their words or views from the heart.

Serving dinner at programs is always very popular. I try not to serve a meal while people are speaking. Of course, when people eat, their full concentration is on food, so why waste the time and plan a working lunch when people only want to work on their cheese sandwich? The menu can be incorporated as part of the program. Lighter meals are great when a program is following the meal. Heavier meals are better when the meal is the close of the event. Remember, the meal should follow closely to the presentation. Many times, I ask the wait staff to leave during presentations so guests can concentrate on the program.

I must say I went to a presentation and I enjoyed having the waitstaff in the room. The speaker made an announcement that if anyone would like to have a glass of water or extra coffee "then just point to your glass." When I pointed to my water glass, the waiter quickly came by, filled my glass and returned to the back of the room. This event showed great service. This was risky because for every glass being filled more noise was added to the presentation. Depending on the event, you must decide whether you want the waitstaff to be present.

People often ask me about how to work with volunteers. One year, I was planning a graduation where I needed several volunteers to handle a group of over four thousand people. Well, 22 volunteers did not show up. This included one person who led the graduates into the arena. Out of 400 faculty, only 75 attended. When I asked the volunteers for simple requests, they could not deliver. The madness had to end. The following year I developed a senior volunteer program. These individuals had to apply for the position. They received perks, such as a gift cards or a personalized t-shirt. Senior volunteers had stars on their collar specifying rank. The senior volunteer job was a recruiting gig. Each senior had to recruit five people to work on their team. Each team was to have one-hundred percent accuracy and delivery on the event. Each senior volunteer carries the freedom of collecting volunteers for his or her team. Each volunteer signs a contract, which states he or she could be dropped as a volunteer at any time. The last thing any company needs is a space holder. Once the team was formulated, I threw a "Let's Perform Well" rally. This is an informal meet and greet. The jobs are laid out and explained. I encourage the group to make it fun and exciting.

Think of all the unique techniques an event planner can develop to host his or her own group rally. The rally could have a theme. If budget is low for the rally, have everyone bring a box of cookies or popcorn. During the planning process, the senior volunteers can submit ideas or complaints on behalf of their group. It is important to know the truth about a situation before it results in people not attending the event.

At the conclusion of the volunteer service, senior volunteers can recommend future seniors. Don't forget to have a concluding volunteer party where each person is given a certificate and is recognized. The senior volunteer should have nothing but nice words to say. The group that had the most team spirit would be given the senior team pin to wear as part of its uniform for next year. Pretty soon, each person will be well-decorated. It is important that the event planner knows who he or she is working with, and the importance that each person carries the experience and energy needed to help.

In college, I volunteered at local hospitals. The hospital facility carried guidelines and expectations. I had to fill out an application; I had a background check and weekly evaluations. This procedure eliminated enlisting the wrong help and decreasing the value of the job.

The smallest bit of help matters. Consider volunteer levels. Each level will require a certain amount of hours. One person may have one hour to spare, so this level may be called the "Emerald Helpers." Select unique names that work well for your event. If I can only cut ribbon for the event, then I can be considered a "diamond" volunteer. Everybody is still valuable.

It is important that people do not stand in the way of your successful event. You need to learn how to utilize their ability, or their unique ability. Never have them resign, but just find a less challenging place for them. With every major volunteer position, have a backup, or have two backups. You could have a senior and super senior program. Super seniors may need to rescue the seniors, for any reason. I was caught off guard with having twenty-two missing volunteers, but your senior volunteers should be strong enough to carry the weight.

You As The Planner

Planning is 24/7 but what about YOU?

You are constantly breathing. The carbon dioxide or unwanted air is being released, while fresh air is being transmitted into your lungs and blood stream. However, people do not pay attention to the inhale-exhale process. Not exhaling completely stresses the body. Should we look at life events in the same demeanor? Keep in mind, events can increase heart rates and tense muscles. Events can also impact your mental well-being. The coping mechanism is known as the BREATHE method:

Break; stop what you are doing
Restore your
Energy and Give
Time for
Healing
Expeditiously

BREATHE is a three step process:
1. Identify the problem: Accepting a new event assignment can be considered the problem.
2. Solve the problem: Be the planner and become the planner.
3. Reward yourself: Successful event outcome results in BREATHE or giving yourself time to prepare for the next undertaking.

I'm sure you're asking:

"How do I fit BREATHE into my hectic schedule?"

Trust me; I understand. During my event season, I average 60-80 events a year.

"How do I select the correct BREATHE to alleviate stress?"

Trust me; you will know because you will stop and inhale deeply like there is a bed of roses in front of you.

Planning to BREATHE

Resign from breaking on or near a holiday. Some holidays produce more stress than an average work day. Plus, certain holidays produce an image. For example, the Fourth of July, beaches are crowded, restaurants could have a longer wait time for seating and the list goes on. This is your day. You create a day that does not make sense to anybody but you.

As you plan your BREATHE, listen to your complaints. In my case, I constantly complain about people not understanding the role of an event planner. I am tired of picking up shrimp shells from banquet seats after a gala. I hate new assignments on a Friday afternoon.

Now, how do I solve my dilemmas? "Do I just do as I am told (majority of the time)?" "Do I implode (majority of the time)?" Or do I say crazy things: "I bet if I ran away and joined the circus (all the time)."

If you could break right now, where would you go? I have always imagined going to Italy and sitting at a sidewalk café on an idle Tuesday afternoon having a warm cappuccino.

I am fine with specifying dreams that are big or ridiculous, because I know I am the planner of my life as well as the planner for others. This daydream can be literal or fictitious. Finding an authentic Italian restaurant in a nearby city or state is feasible. Learning Italian on my way to and from planning meetings is feasible.

On a weight-loss television program, after a team lost a substantial amount of weight, the reward was a night on the town or going to a theme park. Think of your reward in the same way.

Your reward is a combination of your pipe dreams. Living out your pipe dreams will help you BREATHE. For example, I want to run away and join the circus, so I am going to figure out how to make that happen. Hard to take seriously, right? I want to sit at a sidewalk café. Can I really make this happen? The answer is yes. I carry that power and planning ability. Later, I'll tell you about my weekend with the circus!

Trust me; fear of doing a project like this is understandable. However, when you get back to work on Monday morning and your coworkers ask about your vacation, you will have plenty to say. One weekend, I decided to sightsee the city I lived in via helicopter.

I flew through the air with the greatest of ease, as I was a woman on the flying trapeze.

I drove to a bed and breakfast where the innkeeper greeted me by first name: "Good afternoon, Alicia." I watched a sunset over the mountains.

Doesn't this sound too good to be true? Most people say they can't make this happen. Guess what? You are the planner and you know how to make these life events happen. Can you list the things you are tired of, the things that annoy you, and the things you want to change? I bet if you started this list, you would have enough pages to begin a novel.

At a young age, I would challenge myself to work hard to be rewarded. My birthday is in September, so I would work hard from the first day of school until my birthday. My reward was a birthday party, presents and fun with friends. Then I would work hard from my birthday to Halloween. Yes, free candy day. The next holidays in November and December brought nothing but excitement. January would roll around and during the last six months of school, my life was filled with work. The reason for my existence was to understand why Johnny fell down the hill in our reading groups. I wasn't interested. My mind was not involved. Between school and housework, nothing else mattered. I felt I had to let time pass in order to complete the school year. I carried no motivation.

I was working without a reason. Remember in the beginning of the book when I mentioned all the opportunities I had as an event planner, and the numerous offers I rejected? I was a running stream with no end in sight to the repetition of the constant flow.

Even in grade school, the reward brought new motivation to work harder and wiser for a short period of time, and when the rewards ceased, I lost focus and meaning for positive direction. Early in the semester, my restored energy changed my robotic behavior, but later in the semester I was burnt out. My situation equaled my outcome. Boredom and non-reward era resulted in lower grades and lack of motivation.

Wishes to reality was one of my best discoveries. I carry the power to make the necessary changes from ordinary to extraordinary. Even with knowing this bit of information, I learned wishes into reality is equivalent to planning and executing. As I was working hard the month of September to reward myself with a fabulous birthday party, I was *Working through the Process* of the expected assignments from the school. It was hand in hand. Similar to learning Italian and going to an event meeting. I was *Working through the Process*. The rewards broke the redundant behavior.

Grasping mini opportunities built my self-worth. I am determined as a planner to learn how to make the puzzle, build the puzzle, put the puzzle together, see the picture the puzzle offers and celebrate the journey. When the celebration was in existence, I was practicing self-restraint. I was pressurizing my mood, emotions and behavior, which was not healthy. The BREATHE method became a necessity. My ambition to accept projects and events was not adding to my sanity. Keep in mind as a planner, all plans, failure and success are under your control, even when mistakes are not your fault. Placing the super woman cape on my back was not bringing me additional powers but drained my holistic self.

I had to downsize each event to its smallest elements to make the event manageable. The same LOVEE I used for others is the same LOVEE I gave myself. This is how I achieved power. Planners are great at helping others but struggle with motivating themselves as the inspiration fades. When I "L" for one, I "L" for myself. When I "O" for one, I "O" for myself. And so on and so forth.

What if you asked God to break from the event madness? A day you can call your own. How would you plan it? Who would be involved? Do you believe you have the power to make this happen?

When I think about these questions, I get inspired. Who is in control of your life? Is it a close friend? Your job? The money you earn? Think about it.

One Tuesday afternoon, I decided to take my lunch break and go home. As I was walking to my car, I looked up at the sky and realized how beautiful the day was. My office did not have windows, so I was deprived of Mother Nature. I stopped and thanked God for everything, both good and bad. Long days and exhaustion were worth my rewards.

When I got back to work, I suddenly felt the earth move. It was an earthquake. Virginia last recorded a tremor over a century. The earthquake scared several people. I prayed for the safety of others, however I was actually content with the moving earth. I knew I had a full and wonderful life because of my planning. And the best part was, it was all because I had taken time to recognize myself. Yes, it took an earthquake to shake some reality in me.

Imagine you are in a race, but no one else is running. Do you see any problem with this situation? Of course, the effort is diminished because the winner has already been identified. These are the people who die with the experience of just traveling from one city to another without taking the time to go outside their home state. Trust me, the best race is rewarding yourself at the end, because you made the effort.

When preparing your event, take your pipe dream and list all of the components you will need to make it happen: sunglasses, suitcase, bowling ball. At this point, don't factor the time off from work, nor the budget. These considerations could scare yourself away from the actual trip/activity.

For example, I dream of reading my own book at an upscale restaurant. This will require preparation. I will need a dress, shoes, makeup and a completed book. Now each component will become its own category. Do I want a long dress or short dress? What color? For each category, I complete my own research and place my ideas in a binder and place tabs for each section. You should do the same. You will find the research to be just as uplifting as the trip. The research builds excitement.

Once you have the categories, begin doing your research. The internet works well. Use key words to search for information, no matter how silly you may think they are. The search will end with results containing information from people who had similar dreams. Trust me, you are not the only person who has thought of doing this. Remember my dream of running away with the circus? Well, my first step in turning that dream into reality began with typing "joining the circus in Virginia/Washington DC" into the search engine. With this entry, I came across several locations that were in driving distance and cost less than anticipated.

Yes, I ran away with the circus, and my specialty was the flying trapeze. I found the school about three hours away from coastal Virginia. Because of the short distance, I could have taken a 10 a.m. class and been back on the road by noon or could have spent the rest of the day as a tourist.

After the initial research, think about your budget. If you save $20 per month, you will have $360 to play with after one year. (The flying trapeze class was only $40 per session.)

This is your time to be creative. Think about how I plan to celebrate my new book; breaking bread while experiencing fine dining. What is your definition of a fine dining establishment? Can home be my restaurant? What about getting all dressed up, walking down my staircase and being served? What about making a one-of-a-kind dinner and packing it in an executive case and renting a chauffeured car for $50 an hour and enjoying delectable delights as I tour the city? Keep all your options in your notebook. Now select an option that is right for you and your budget.

Every scenario and minute step is a goal that needs to be accomplished. Love is in the details, right?

Once you have completed your planning, place your categories in the order of importance. In my case, I may own a dress that may be acceptable; therefore, spending the money on a new one may not be necessary. Once I meet one goal, I can make sure I start conquering the rest of my list in the order of importance.

Capture the moment. I am a true believer in journaling. Write down your feelings toward preparing for the reward. Take pictures and post them where you can remember the wonderful things you have done and created. If you own a shop or have a desk, display the pictures. Trust me; it will encourage others to do the same. In my office, I have pictures of my flying trapeze excursion. My display also includes a photo of me holding a baby tiger and playing with the Berenstain Bears (another long story).

Let's look at another mission. Let's say, between work and children, your life does not see daylight. Your pipe dream is for you to have the house to yourself. You deserve that reward. What if you hired a cleaning service, a personal chef to make you lunch and a personal assistant to screen your calls, while you sleep in your king-size bed by yourself? Do you think this scenario would make you take a breath? Of course it would.

If your reward is to have a cleaning service detail your home, pretend this is of the norm. Sit back and watch your house get transformed from a dust bunny's paradise to squeaks of clean.

Occasionally when I plan reward events, I pretend the occasion/experience was a gift or surprise. In fact, it is a surprise. Not knowing the taste of food or the personalities of the housekeepers makes the experience mystery profound. This planning manual is a keepsake from a day of enjoyment.

Another way to plan activities is through your bucket list. We all have a bucket list, and it is intimidating to consider; however, very few plan to the caliber of concurring lifelong aspirations. Your goal is to plan experiences that are novel in nature. Knowing that your mind is a file, you are one step ahead of the vision to revision phase.

Keep telling yourself, "Don't be scared!" You get one shot in life. What are you going to do with it?

I must tell you this story. A very good friend never had a BREATHE. It is something that people just don't do. A normal date night was dinner and a movie, so he decided to do a reward adventure. He spent a little under a year planning this event. He did as I advised and created a manual, a timeline, a budget report and categories. He set a goal, which was to hang glide over a sand dune. He was a beginner in this process; however, he did very well and was successful in his outcome — that's why I married him.

I must make this disclaimer about inviting people on these reward journeys. Ask yourself, "Is the person accompanying me worthy of this adventure?" Remember, he or she is getting a free ride off of your reward. Is this your preference? If so, I suggest interviewing the person before you ask them to partake in your experience. As I mentioned in the previous chapter, take the person's emotions into consideration then document emotion comparisons.

For example, what if your favorite food is pizza, and your invited guest is allergic to pizza sauce? Will you be disappointed if your invited guest could not experience the great flavors with you? Are you apt to change your plans to satisfy another? Think about it.

Understand it is acceptable to take separate adventures. If pasta sauce is your favorite and you are dying to taste a new pizza, find out what other restaurants are near and go your separate ways. Even a trip for two should be about you. Your likes will not always be the likes of others. Just learn to meet your goal and keep moving.

Once you have all the information of the locations and activities, print all of your agreements/ contracts. Use your contracts to create a timeline.

Your personal timeline will be a little different. You must keep yourself in order. Give yourself plenty of time to make it from one appointment to the next.

4:00 p.m. Iron my dress
4:20 p.m. Cleanse face for makeup
5:00 p.m. Leave house and journey toward restaurant

I know this may seem too detailed, but you don't want to miss out on your reward.

Be true to yourself. When you enter a project of this stature, you know who your naysayers are. Many times, during my self-improvement planning and my reward planning, my plan is my secret. You will come across more negative people in this world than positive.

> Never have anyone step on a dream or life mission.

You carry the power for improvement and success. When I sit in that restaurant as the author of my first book, no one can take that BREATHE away from me. What is meant for me is for me.

Always take into account A+B+C. Be proud of A. Be even more proud of B. Give thanks when you accomplish C. Write down your steps for your success track and stick to the plan. Think about your BREATHE method. Make it worth accomplishing your goals.

I look at these adventures and rewards as my treasure in my treasure chest. Consider your adventures as God's way of blessing you.

One more note: When you are partaking in your reward, don't screw it up. It only takes one second to turn a great day into the most horrific experience of the year. Remember the rules and laws of the city and know your personal rules and laws. In other words, remember your morals. Do not challenge yourself to experience anything that may be unsafe.

I Tracks: Tracking and planning
your personal goals

I must admit when I tried my BREATHE plan for the first time, I was motivated, I was inspired and I failed. I regrouped and developed a tracking system called "I Tracks," which is defined as keeping track of the success progress.

I began using I Tracks with two smaller goals: not eating junk food in the evening hours and reading one chapter a night. By week two, I was back to eating a half of bag of chips and my book turned into a late night movie. I was very disappointed in myself. I carried the desire for change but not the drive to complete a goal. It was baffling why I could not follow my own plan. I had several discussions with others who had a similar problem. We could write the problem, and we could solve the problem on paper, but we had no idea that the solution was more than a thought put on paper; it was about action that was evolving. Changing one habit was not enough power to keep the engine operating. Determining that chips at 3 a.m. was not a healthy habit is not enough. It is determining why you are awake at 3 a.m., why you are hungry at 3a.m. and why chips. These thoughts meant I had to change my lifestyle as a whole. Think about it: when you move your leg, it takes muscles, nerves and your brain to make your leg move two inches to the left. Changing one habit was not enough, nor was it effective, for me. I started I tracking my day, everything I did from sunup to sundown. I changed several aspects of my life. If I started my day with a cup of coffee, I changed the coffee to a cup of tea. If I enjoyed two cookies before bed, I changed my two cookies to a cup of raisins. In other words, I changed my "track," or I changed my running course. Everything needed to change. Changing one or two courses of action was hard, changing almost everything was harder, but my lifestyle change made the best impact. The smaller components that I struggled with were now the easier ones. I was making several small moves that resulted in shifting to a new norm.

With my 180 degree behavioral change, I had to think before making any move. After two weeks of my new I Track, I documented my current situation and guess what I made? Another full change of habits. Why, you may ask. So I would not become complacent in my actions. My actions for three months were never the norm, but always my new norm. My body had to prepare for constant change.

You have breakable habits. Your transition is comparable to an ugly vase. Place the vase in your hands. Now lift the vase over your head and throw it to the ground. The bigger the problem, the bigger the vase; the louder the sound, the more pieces it shatters into. It is nearly impossible for you to glue it back together. Isn't that great? Isn't the sound fantastic?

Think of your life events as a thermostat. On a hot summer day, you set your thermostat to sixty-five degrees. It takes forever for your thermostat to equal the temperature in the room, but it happens. The cooling system allows it to happen. In your life events, the situation may feel uncomfortable, but you are not done controlling the temperature.

When I was going through my I Tracks, I knew I could not adjust my habits once a week. Somedays I needed to adjust hourly. Yes, every hour.

I started to document every hour and sometimes minute of my day. One hour equaled three pages of documentation. That was fine with me. I was on a mission. I really wanted to brag to myself that I made it happen. This is bad to say, but my A+B+C was more like. A.1+A.2+A.3. It did not matter in my life how long I was making bad habits; the quest was how far did I need to lift my arms to make a loud enough vase crashing noise to startle me into never having that habit again? Keep telling yourself that this is your new year, and your new year can start on any date on the calendar.

Once I made constant changes, I adjusted to the change. The original mission was accomplished in the midst of changing everything else. After three months, I celebrated by spending the day at the beach.

I once knew a woman who was suffering from depression. I explained to her how to use I Tracks. I advised her to plan rewards. Every Tuesday was "Coffee by the Fountain" reward day. Every Wednesday was "Walk at a Park thirty minutes Away from Home" day, and Friday was "New Restaurant" day or "Create a Food Masterpiece" day. This woman's mission was for her to physically understand that she could change her daily habits. I call this "The Santa Claus View." You believe you are trapped until you see yourself that you are not. Don't forget "nothing exists unless it is documented." Document how it feels to have your first cup of coffee and then your first visit to the park. Document your senses, and tell yourself to "let your life happen."

I learned that I needed to value my time. With the amount of time I was spending on others, I was undervaluing myself. With I Tracks, I was able to reexamine my life on paper. My learning curve was not wasting time, and I had options. Our value system tells us that if we help others, our lives will be fulfilled, and I agree. Many people would like to give; however, they lack the time and money. If you overextend yourself, you will be stressed because the balance of helping others and helping yourself is just not where it should be. Again, this can lead to sickness or exploding. Trust me: this is a good way to become a poor role model.

A friend recently joined an organization that required community outreach. The more he did in the community, the more popular he became. In the meantime, he almost lost his home to foreclosure, and his marriage became rocky. He needed a wakeup call on helping others.

What is "soul" to you? Soul could be your innermost being. It could be a connection to God. Soul could be your mind. What if your soul was undefined because you could not express it? You could not speak. Maybe you can't listen. The only vehicle of expression that you have is your eyes. Could you read someone's soul only through his or her eyes? Your eyes could depict happiness, sorrow, worry or exhaustion, but your eyes do not express the reasons why. Either way, I needed my definition of SOUL.

Stop
Observe
Understand
Listen

I mentioned the key in planning success is interviewing. Now how are you going to receive information if the people you are working with are mute? Your supervisor tells you to read medical charts to get background history, but there is not a chart in this world that will express the soul. So I had to learn to Stop, Observe, Understand and Listen.

Early on in my health care event planning days, I asked a staff member who the cream of the crop event planner at the facility. A name was given to me, and I went to the floor on which she worked. I saw a room decorated for a birthday party. There were helium balloons as centerpieces. The napkins were neatly folded with forks placed on the napkins. Everything was very uniform. I watched the activities coordinator wheel in the residents and place them next to the tables. Next a woman with a guitar played the song "I'll Fly Away." Then a sugar-free cake was served, and the party was over.

During my SOUL, I noticed the plane had crashed before it had even taken off. If I am sitting in a wheel chair, would I see the décor even existed? Remember helium balloons are not at eye level. Then, at a birthday party the performer sings about death. Some of the patients nodded off to sleep, and the others were looking forward to the sugarless cake.

The next day, I thanked the event planner for allowing me to partake in the resident's celebration. I did question the décor. "Why helium balloons?" I asked. The planner mentioned the budget was low, and the only items provided by the facility were multicolored balloons. For St Patrick's Day, green balloons; orange balloons for Halloween; and can you guess what color balloons were used for the Christmas party?

As mentioned in Chapter One, your mind is a file, and the first time you experience any occasion, you will remember it. Now think about seeing the same décor for a different party. Let me tell you a little story of what happened to me.

For the next birthday party, I was asked by the balloon galore planner to gather residents for another birthday celebration. I knocked on a resident's door and told her that a party was starting in ten minutes, so she grabbed her purse and slowly walked down the hallway. Every minute she would call my name. "Excuse me, Miss. Where did you say that party was?" I told her that it was in the common area, so she kept walking. About a minute later, she called for me again. "Excuse me, Miss. Where is that party?" I told her again that it was in the common area. This time I noticed that she was standing in the middle of the room with the balloons surrounding her and the same happy birthday sign. I listened to her mumble underneath her breath, "Now where is that damn party!" I guess she had seen the balloons so many times that it blended in with the furniture. Okay, I laughed, not at her, but because it was time for a change.

Two months later, I was tasked with planning the party for the residents.

My first step was to research décor on a budget. Keeping in mind that the décor is an environment change, I knew there were many factors to consider. To solve the problem, I would go outside and cut fresh flowers. I would place the flowers on the party tables at eye level.

I had to do some manipulation with the balloons. I contacted a local clown who showed me the ins and outs of balloon décor. To solve the balloon problem, I placed the décor at two levels, wheelchair view and higher for residents who could stand. I would strategically place the helium balloons on the ceiling where residents would see only the ribbon hanging in front of them when the residents would get wheeled in. This encouraged the residents to lift up their arms and move the ribbon out of their way, which is a range of motion exercise. I observed several residents looking up at all the ribbons on the ceiling. Remember, not only is this exercise, but a form of communication. If you walked into a party space, and there was one piece of ribbon dangling in front of you, would you be annoyed? Would you be happy about it? There was plenty for them to talk about.

"Hey, Alicia, this annoys me."

"Hey, this is fun!"

Another mission that I wanted to accomplish was to eradicate the mention of death at any event. I understand that entertainers can be pricy, and if you can get a free one, why not go for it? However, sometimes free is not worth the money and the results. The ever so popular song "I'll Fly Away" had to stop. I did my research and came across an entertainment company sponsoring a performer who sang music from the 1920s and 1930s. The price, $250 per hour, was considered expensive. I knew it was worth it.

When the party began, I noticed that the residents sat straight up. They clapped along with the music. One resident even started to dance. At the end of the performance, everyone in the room gave the singer a standing ovation or raised his or her arms and applauded. A few of the residents went to thank the balloon décor galore planner for allowing the performer to entertain for this birthday party. At this birthday party, the flowers, balloons and singer were the environment changer.

This event gave the residents a new smile and a new reason not to "Fly Away." The residents understood that great things come in all events. Deviation is great, and accepting new experiences is even better. After the first event that I planned, the residents accepted the change. Even though I no longer work at the retirement center, some events have been grandfathered in as annual special occasions.

Remember SOUL.

Stop. Do not make any adjustment to event dynamics until you have all the documentation indicating a change is needed.

Observe the normal routine and take notes on behaviors of others, just observe the normal routine. Because most events happen only once a year, the routine may be hard to observe. You are responsible for retrieving all information to produce an image of the event.

Understand. Restate what you understand about the event. Provide an epi report of last year's event and your recommended changes for this year's event. Have supporting data. Is there a survey after each event that indicates a need for change?

Listen for feedback. Understand the opinions of others and decide which battles you are willing to fight, whether it is for the client or the positive reflection upon the company.

As an event planner, you will be challenged by family and friends to create the best event ever for little or no money. In the beginning, this could be fun, and the attention from your supporting fans can be uplifting. But I have learned my lesson. I am a true believer that family comes first; however, making arrangements for an event must be a two-way street. Spend the same amount of time, or additional planning time, for your family's events as you would a client who is paying you.

I had to create a rule for myself, which I called my EEE. Every event that I plan for a family member or friend must be Experimental, Educational and Elastic. I know this sounds a little selfish. However, the event must benefit me.

The positive side to planning an event for your family or friends is you are able to *experiment* with event designs on a smaller scale. One of my favorite designs came from a dinner party I coordinated for friends. I love bugs, and I wanted to incorporate live butterflies in my tablescape (table setup). Many companies wouldn't allow me to use this unique butterfly design, so after my experimentation and several awesome pictures of my creation, I was able to sell my design to three brides. I was able to recoup my investment in the experiment. I once heard of a company that sold unique crumb cakes in the area. For a friend's birthday, I hired the company. Well, the cake showed up two hours late. I called the vendor several times, and the calls went straight to voicemail. When the cake arrived, I could tell that it was a rush job. I did not pay for the cake; however, I learned not to recommend this company to other clients. I also did a similar experiment about three years ago and ordered a birthday cake from a new company. This vendor was absolutely fabulous. I receive one free cake a year because of the amount of business I give her. Some experiments are positive. Others are negative.

Educational refers to practicing designs that I have not completed in the past. Also, I may use a vendor I have never used. Therefore, my friends will become the guinea pigs for sampling new food or viewing new designs. Educational also includes research on the event industry. Finding out what the new trends are and learning how to manipulate them into your own design work can be challenging. One design that is popular is a "lounge" event. Loosely speaking, a lounge could be nothing more than your living room. What if you rented soft blue gel lighting and added fresh flowers? You will have created the ever-so-popular "lounge."

The last E stands for *Elastic*. Elastic is used in clothing because it adjusts to the fit of the person. The "clothing" is the details of the event, and that person is me. The family member or friend must adjust to me, whether I need funding for the event or a certain amount of time to work the event into my schedule. I must choose the date that works well for me, or I must be able to design as I please. As I mentioned, if I am giving up my time, energy and talents, I think this is a fair compromise.

For example, I was asked to decorate for a baby shower. I gave a list of all the supplies that I needed to the party host. Then I looked at the theme of the event and came up with a design that would fit my friend's personality. This design offered me the opportunity for education and a chance to experiment. Lastly, I placed my name on everything that I designed. This is a marketing tool for me. If you are an awesome planner, which I know you are, your family and friends will probably feel pleased with an original design.

43

The Power of Giving Back

I keep a log of all vendors that I have worked with, all the money I have pushed their way and all the services that they have provided. At the end of the year, sometimes, I will send them an Action Update Report. In the letter, I will thank them for their services and state, "This year, X number of money or clients were sent your way." The vendor typically responds with a coupon for a free service or a discounted service. Well, I believe in giving back, so I forward the offers to a client in need.

In another example, my mother had a Sunday dinner tradition, which involved her cooking a large home-cooked meal, my sister bringing empty bowls to the house to collect leftovers and grandchildren playing freely. One Sunday, I overheard my mother stating that preparing the dinner was hard work, and she needed a break.

One December morning, I planned for a private chef to prepare a family dinner at my parent's home. My mother also made comments about having a family portrait, I arranged for another vendor to take pictures of the dinner experience along with a family portrait.

As I mentioned in a previous chapter, listen to yourself as you make requests. Write down what you are stating and make it happen. Two months later, my mother developed an illness in which she lost her hair and taste buds. What if I had waited to plan this dinner or I had never acted on her remark?

As a planner, I learned to keep an event piggy bank. If an event is placed on your heart, especially if it is for family, make it happen.

During the time of my mother's diagnosis, the family walked around with a gray cloud over their heads. It was hard to handle the day-by-day news and remain smiling. Unfortunately, the announcement of my mother's medical concerns occurred around her fortieth wedding anniversary. My sister and I had planned a big surprise, which we had to cancel immediately. My sister and I spent hours on the phone talking about a perfect gift, and none seemed to fit despite the situation.

Then it hit me. I hadn't been listening to my own expertise. I hadn't been using the information I deliver in seminars that I've taught or included in articles that I've written. I needed an environment change. I needed to take the surroundings and make them pleasant again. In my setup, I knew I needed to use the stimuli that affect the five senses.

One night, my husband suggested we have a stilt walker outside juggling when my mother arrived home from church. My husband has always claimed that I know everybody, so, yes, I do know a traveling stilt walker who juggles.

One day after church, my sister placed her two young children in the back seat of my mom's car. The children love to ride to Grandma's house.

I could see my mom pull up slowly. She stopped the car in the middle of the street in amazement to see a juggler on her front lawn. On the house was a sign that read "Happy 40th Wedding Anniversary." She pulled up into the driveway and started laughing. Once my mom and the kids got out of the car, the kids pulled on Grandma's skirt, pointing and making sure she did not miss a beat of the juggling act.

After the act, my parents had to fish their way through a sea of helium balloons, tacky paper bells and streamers located inside the home. According to wedding pictures, these were the decorations my parents used for their wedding reception, so, in this case, the more stimuli, the better. My goal was to create a new "file." My parents touching ribbons and pulling streamers down to get into their house was exercising the sense of touch. The juggler was sight.

My wonderful husband prepared old-fashioned BBQ to stimulate their sense of taste. I know that some of my mom's greatest memories are sitting outside, laughing, at a BBQ. Adding this one to her "file" was challenging because she has so many experiences in this setting. Therefore, I needed to put a spin on the food. My husband served Jerk/teriyaki chicken, warm potato salad, green bean casserole and homemade iced tea. The meal was plentiful and delicious.

During the next couple of days, my mother traveled back and forth regularly to the hospital. My sister and I noticed that during her all-day medical appointments, she was having fast food for breakfast, lunch and dinner. My mother loves to shop, but did not have the time. One day, before she came home from the doctor's office, my sister and I redid the decorations in the house and decorated the hallway with $600 worth of gift cards. With the gift cards, she could shop online, pay for gas and use them at every restaurant and fast food place you could think of. She was very appreciative.

The following Christmas, I hosted another gathering where my mother and the rest of my family could break bread and give thanks for making it through the year. That year, they learned, events can change the emotions of the current situation and make them better. The December event was a reward gift — a BREATH — for making it through and sticking together.

44

One Tuesday afternoon, I took the time to look throughout my storage closet only to find a room filled with décor that had not been used for years. I thought about giving away the items (or putting them in the trash). However, before acting on my thoughts, I took a SOUL break. I stopped, observed, understood and listened. Many times in life, you need to listen to your thoughts. I decided to hold on to the items. Here's the reason why:

Several years ago, I was hired to plan a children's birthday party. Not only did this mother hire a planner, but she had bounce houses, clowns, games and activities. This children's birthday party was way over $1,000. When I was younger, I was just excited that my friend had matching plates.

My thoughts were leading me in the direction of the children who may not have the opportunity to have such a childhood experience. So I came up with an idea to find local parents who were having a hard time keeping up with the trends of a childhood birthday party.

Using my vendor reports and the update action reports, I contacted all the cake designers that I have given a substantial amount of business to and asked if they would be willing to donate birthday cakes. All of my cake designers loved the idea that their cakes would be given to children in need. Knowing I had free birthday cakes and a closet full of décor, I started a charity called "Shhh, It's a Secret." Local social workers talked to parents about the service, and a few parents contacted me with information about their children. The parents had two options: they could pick up the items, or I would donate my time and plan games and activities at no charge.

This was a great experience for the children because they were able to keep up with their friends as far as social gathering, and the children had no clue that the event was through my service. That was a secret between the parents and me.

There is another service that many clowns and entertainers are known for. They travel to children's hospitals. As a planner, be well-rounded by showing the industry how planners have helped others. Keep in mind that the service that you provide is a positive one.

Uniqueness is the Key

As an event planner, you will receive invitations to charity balls and donation dinners and the list goes on. I heard of an event planner who specialized in non-gala galas. You receive the invitation in the mail. For example, the invite may say:

Date: March 6, 20XX
Time: 7:00 p.m.
Location: Ben's Hotel, in Highland City
Purpose: Raise money for the softball league
Dress: Your pajamas
Food: Whatever you have in your fridge or take out
Entertainment: Your favorite TV show or possibly a movie

Attendance is not needed, just pay the money. The date and time of the event is actually the deadline for donations. You can receive sponsorships and sell tables and plates, but think about all the overhead you are not paying for! The invites and thank you cards are the only costs for the fundraiser. The next time you plan an event, compare the overhead with the money actually earned. It is important to raise money from the ticket sales as well as the sponsorships. If the ticket sales pay only for the event, then consider raising the cost of the table or per plate value or have a non-gala gala. Each person who pays is considered your attendance cost.

When I plan galas, I try to keep the cost down with the décor, entertainment and food. It may seem dull. However, the best part of the evening is an idea called The Dessert Extravaganza. During dinner, the dessert is not placed on the table. Instead, it is placed in a separate room. During a special time of the evening, the guests parade into a dessert room, which is themed with décor, lights, special effects and dessert flambé stations. The room is small, and the food is served buffet style. All the guests are wowed by this. (This also works as your "five percent from your childhood. All events should be 5% childish") People walk away from the event thrilled because of the dessert room. Trust me; you will start a new "file" with this presentation.

The Power of the Flower

I had a conversation with a friend about her elderly mother who had become ill. The friend, also an event planner, had a different remedy for healing.

After my friend spent several days by her mother's side, a doctor approached her with the disturbing news that her mother's life was ending. Because she was on life support in ICU, my friend's mother was in an environment that was filled with plugs and machines, but my planner friend did not let that jar her inner super planner. She started planning a theme party for her mother as a celebration-of-life shindig.

Her party location was the ICU room where her mother was located. My friend broke all the rules and regulations in place in order to protect the patient. She bought three dozen helium balloons, flowers, cake and a band into the ICU room.

She themed the party "Put on the Red High Heel Shoes," which came from the movie "The Wizard of Oz." My friend was inspired by the scene in which Dorothy clicks her heels three times and says, "There is no place like home." Everyone invited was requested to wear red shoes. Even the men were provided with a red high heel pin, which they wore on their lapel.

During the event, songs and laughter filled the

ICU party. My friend noticed that her mother was tapping her foot to the beat of the music. Her head moved like she was looking at the décor, but never did her eyes open. People gave testimonies about the mother and gave her great praise for her life.

When the party was over, the daughter asked the nurse to remove the life support and give her mother oxygen. She sat by her mother as her mother opened her eyes and gave a bright smile using only her eyes. Doctors mentioned that this could be a reflex, but my friend took this as a sign of appreciation and love. Later that night, her mother passed away. My friend was pleased with the sendoff.

One piece of advice about event planning: it takes time to advance within the profession. This time is extensive time: from late nights to early mornings. On a Saturday afternoon, I was adoring pictures on Facebook. A dear friend posted pictures of a pond with ducks playing in the water. Another photo was a picture of birds in the air, and the last picture — that grabbed my heart strings — was a picture of autumn leaves.

I could not believe everything that I was missing. I really had to think about what in my life was important. Was it the designs and long hours or the balance of work and life that were prudent? My days consisted of reading files, restocking décor, backaches from lifting tablecloths and running on auto pilot.

Looking at all the pictures of events I had planned, they sure make great wall pieces, but what I had to learn was to create wall pieces of my personal life — like my nephews getting ready for school or taking a surprise picture of my mom. I believe in hard work, and I believe in the dedication to make it in this industry. However, something must give. I love my Sundays, and that is the day I choose for myself. Of course, events can happen on a Sunday, so, sometimes, I must substitute my Sunday with another break day.

During my years of planning, I must admit I learned about myself. The years of parades, weddings and galas are what my heart desires as a career. My love is also a starry night, a home that is filled with love and again me holding a cup of coffee and seeing life through the many years that I have helped others. I see myself training for a marathon and losing a few pounds. I see myself picking up babies and rocking them to sleep in hospitals. I see myself accepting the beam of happiness and doing whatever I can to make it grow. I also see myself getting through life's challenges without falling apart and learning how to react properly. Planners are about pleasing others and yourself.

Event planners are everywhere. As I mentioned, the number of Santa's on every street corner is equivalent to the number of event planners. After letting down my guard and accepting that planners can work together, I accepted an offer to help plan an event for celebrity event planner David Tutera. I was not the lead, just a person willing to help as needed. When I arrived at the event location, I was asked several questions by planners: my name, where I lived and whether I had experience in designing. I made sure I answered each question with a smile. After hours of decorating, nature called, and I decided to take a bathroom break. While in the stall, I heard a young voice at my door.

"Hello?"

"Yes?" I replied, hoping she was just asking me for some tissue.

"Humm... I have been watching you decorate. Where are you from and what is the name of your business?"

Really?

Seriously?

Is this young woman part of some event planning gang that decided to corner me in the bathroom?

As I flushed the toilet, she continued to ask me questions. "How long have you been in the business?"

This young woman even followed me to the sink, and she asked me about my most popular designs.

When I reached for the paper towel, she left the bathroom. I didn't know how to take this. I could not believe I had fallen in her trap and actually answered the questions, like it was the right thing to do.

Ask yourself, "Why am I an event planner?" Many people choose the profession because they enjoyed planning their wedding or because they helped out at a party or family reunion and now they are hooked. Therefore, only a business card was needed to jumpstart an event planning career. With a business card and one successful event under their belts, every new event will be magic, right? After all, their work is better than other area event planners.

Well, let's examine this scenario. From your first client, you receive a check for $100. In your planning, the bride arrives at the church an hour late. Your excuse is that all weddings start late. Your wedding designs consist of bolts of tulle, curling ribbon and silk flowers. You step back to look at your designs and you are highly impressed, so you think you're an expert, right? Well, as much as you want to be that new event designer and planner, inexperienced planners only hurt the event planning industry.

What are the signs of an inexperienced event planner? How will you know if you have hired one or if you are one?

One of the students in my event-planning workshop showed me a picture similar to the design that I described. Unfortunately, I had some bad news for her. The design shown was popular in 1980. And, no, all weddings do not start late. With proper planning, weddings can start on time.

Experience is the one thing that sets event planners apart. I have worked for companies where the people who interview for the position do not understand the makings of a great planner. I recently sat on an interview board to hire an events coordinator. One of the interviewers on the panel was impressed by the client because she owned her own wedding business. When I asked the interviewee about the steps of planning an event, the answers were not clear. She mentioned nothing about event budgets, providing site surveys, or even generating information on the date and time of the event.

In the event planning market, new planners are in constant need of information. I was working with a bride, who hired two event planners. When I asked the bride to explain her vision for her event, I noticed the planner was taking notes from my notebook. The techniques that I use for organization just happened to show up during our next meeting. Honestly, I have worked very hard to create forms. I knew my information was not safe around other planners. I have even had my designs show up on other planners' websites. The bottom line is when people don't know, they pretend to know.

Not only is information stolen from other planners, but many planners use stock photos from the internet. There is an event planning company in California that sells event planning portfolio pictures. What happens when you see a beautiful event picture? Of course you fall in love with the designer. Again, it hurts the market for people who actually design and pay a photographer to capture the moment. As a client, it is important to research every picture and article that is given to you.

I did an event that required a table lady, a lady who dresses in costume and stands in a hole in the middle of a table with skirting around it. The table acts as the lady's dress. When I contacted the company, they sent me a picture of a wonderful costumed table lady. I was very excited because it was exactly what I was looking for. I asked the planner if the picture was original or a stock photo. The planner claimed that it was her design. Later that night, I was surfing the web for additional information on the table ladies. I happened to come across the same picture from a drag queen website. This drag queen company is top of the line for table ladies and costume characters for events. I quickly contacted the local company via email and continued to ask questions about the image. As the event designer claimed the design was still hers, I still hired the company, knowing that what I was getting was not going to be in the picture. What I received on my event date was not even passable. As an event planner, I could tell the makeup was splotchy, and the costume lacked imagination. What made the problem even worse was the crowd loved the table lady concept!

In this scenario why would the crowd love this table lady? Of course, this was their first exposure to one. This is very similar to beginner planners. Everything is wonderful, but to another planner's eye, not everything is. Now, what would happen if all my guests at the party noticed the flaws that I saw? Think about it. I would have wasted the company's money, and the credibility of the event store would have decreased.

I could not believe that the planner tried to present false information. As a planner, you have to be honest. If you are a beginner, tell the client that this is a learning experience. I was honest with my very first bride. I charged the client gas money and collected a tip. I asked if I could use her pictures for my portfolio and if I could use her as a reference. Even in my contract, I stated that I was a novice planner. It took two years to gain the experience I needed to handle a large wedding with an incredible amount of detail.

What is your stepladder for success? It is hard to find the right information needed to start a planning business. Numerous companies have no idea what proper training is needed, so often, companies ask for background experience in marketing or business. With my event-planning background, what has worked well for me is a background in psychology and business with a concentration in events. I would highly recommend a master's degree. As I have mentioned in this book, events are about changing the environment, proper interviewing and manipulation of everyday life. As an event planner, you will see emotion. I had a bride who went into a depression during the planning stage of her wedding. When I went to a meeting at her house, she was sitting in a dark room, rocking back and forth. The stress of getting married was unbearable, causing a meltdown. Remember, you are not a psychologist. You are, however, a supporter. Knowing how to handle a situation very similar to this can be challenging.

Seventy-five percent of event planning is paperwork, and twenty-five percent is actually the event. Creating memos, proposals, speaking in public and justifying a case will help you in the business aspect of planning. The rest of the knowledge can be self-taught. Ask any designer how they started their business. Many will speak about natural talent. Others will tell you they took a course and ran with it. They were trendsetters and not followers.

The event planning market is competitive because of the inexperienced planners. What has taken me over twenty years to master, an inexperienced planner is claiming to same knowledge. Let's think about a photographer. A photographer works one day taking pictures on location and several hours making sure the photos are perfect. A planner can work 365 days and still not receive the same amount of money as a photographer.

Let's do some math. Let's say a photographer has a $10,000 package deal. If labor for editing and printing the pictures was not taken into account, the photographer and his/her assistant are splitting about $1,250 an hour. On average, that is what many base salary workers earn in two weeks. A wedding planner may charge $10,000 for eight months of work. This planner is getting paid $1,250 per month.

Let's say I want to charge $10,000 for my planning service, and another planner wants to charge $500 for eight months. Which planner would you hire? Many clients have no idea who is experienced and who is not. Therefore, I could be losing my clients and the creditability that this field has. It is important that the planner can offer more than one service. Many planners call themselves wedding planners because that is where the market is. Many neglect to find a market that is not open and make a mark on it, as I did.

Once you comprehend the event planning system, it is time to exercise your knowledge. The best way to showcase your abilities is through a voluntary planned function or social occasion. This noteworthy occurrence should carry event planning components: budget, program, venue, decor and agenda. This partaking must have a complete event cycle or LOVEE. Most importantly, lend feedback from clientele and vendors, consequently generating referrals. Positive testimonies can be used to build a repertoire. Keep in mind, these communications do not have a lifespan.

> A former bride celebrated her 18th wedding anniversary. On social media she reflected on her memorable wedding day. Soon after the comments, I received a request to coordinate a wedding.

Your first venture will explore your strategy in reliable decision making. Log the progress in sections: complexity, plan alterations and interpersonal. This first event is an endeavor, therefore reporting your progress will assist in correcting mistakes on your next undertaking.

Within a few years of starting my career, I began an impact-kudos journal containing compliments from clients and a progression journal outlining my career growth. These journals were pivotal to my sustainability success plan. It was crucial in my new journey, and I didn't damage relationships because of my lack of knowledge and within this exploratory time of my career, I had positive motivation.

When I first began my profession, acceptance was a challenge due to my unique creative process. Documenting a perfectly planned event in my impact-kudos journal was a major accomplishment. It meant I had finally won the hearts of others, and these individuals were my investors. I was progressing, and my judgement was trusted. This journal entry brought energy and motivation to continue to achieve a plan.

A client who hires a new planner may not be able to make a clear judgement on the experience level. The client is looking for an information source who can be trusted. For example, a tick tock, TFO and timeline may not carry meaning. The client is concerned about the progress but NID (not into details). In other words, a client is watching your planning television channel but not reading your script. Make adjustments as needed to your plan. Remember, your body language and punctuality is communicating your new brand.

Your first event planning experience will be similar to a pot of stew. When a pot of stew lingers, the flavors fall apart and could become lackluster, but when you stir it up, the greatness of the soup takes shape. You may be stirred by your first event, but that is when greatness prevails.

You are the master. It is time to plan like you are one. Sometimes taking that first leap of faith, you may feel unqualified. But, trust me, it is in you. I never knew that this gift was in me.

No matter what trouble is showing on the horizon, remain calm and deliver. As a planner, you will need the strength and wisdom to carry through. Your guests should not outrun your creativity with negative responses, and trust me, it only takes one negative comment from a client to downgrade your capabilities. Whether you are defining events as a social atmosphere or you are defining them as part of your life, the makings of your first event should be passable.

Write a list of personal expectations before this commitment. With each expectation write a solution. Be honest with yourself.
1. Sore feet   Solution: extra pair of shoes
2. High Stress   Solution: Picture of a beach in your planning book

After spending seven months planning and designing a gala, upon ordering the last decorating items I received an email stating that the gala decor budget was reduced due to the increased audio visual equipment requested by a senator. My lavish floral design consisting of roses, callas, orchids, hydrangea, leaves and lily grasses was substituted with two roses with baker's fern in each vase. The original lavish arrangement would be pinspotted with a soft white glow. Now I would need several people to point flashlights at tables for the same ambiance.

What happened? My beautiful lighting and florals — gone. The tech equipment took precedence. I understood the need for funding and supported the company's decision, however the event luster was depreciated. I, the planner, had to manipulate conditions despite the situation.

If the company initially budgeted "ten dollars" for environmental change, I would spend "five dollars" the best way I could. I wanted the gala participants to understand the vision was created in the company's best interest. Keep in mind guests are not viewing financial reports, they are experiencing an event with the first impression being decor. The question was, "How can I prove that the years of training and my crystal ball vision can still exist?"

With no money to spare, I made a few calls to local companies and priced the pinspot lights. The lighting orders averaged $1,900. This was a price I was not willing to shell out of my pocket. Another company was trying to help and priced the décor at $500. That proved that I was not doing the research I needed to find a company that would perform services at an extremely low price. But again, with the great price of $500, it was still over budget. How would I answer my supervisor if she questioned how I furnished the lights when the budget did not permit.

Almost giving up, I tried one last quest. I contacted a rental store. This store was able to rent a lighting tree for $11, and the lighting fixtures at $12 each. By the time I totaled the lighting expense, I spent $300 to keep my vision alive. I was sold. I had two problems. The rental company was one hour away, and I had never rigged lighting. I was trained in lighting work, but I never installed a full lighting show. To make a long story short, I had to learn how, and had less than a week to learn. My genius mind contacted a local theater school and requested a light tech to assist. This was a little overboard just to try to make a vision come to life and pinspot roses. I must admit the success was up to me and God. I really prayed for direction. I believe in the complete package: environment change and strong programming.

I must be trained to handle any situation and to know when it is my time to shine and when it is not. With two hundred CEOs and guests in one room, yes, it was my time to shine.

My accidental event planning career turned into a *phenomenon* of successful life changing occurrences. I appreciate all my brides, clients, mentors and mentees who assisted with my planning endeavors. As the world of events evolves, the planning spectrum is being manipulated. This *phenomenon* is developing into a greater *phenomenon*. Paper planning guides are now computer generated spread sheets to include timelines and agendas based on mathematical data.

I applaud the new technology driven industry, which makes becoming an event planner easy. When I first engaged the industry, planners where elite with special skill sets, similar to J Lo in "The Wedding Planner." Today the personal touch is falling short with overbookings and internal industry competition.

Let's not forget the Power of Events. We are not car sales professionals trying to make a sale. We are not in competition with each other. The higher the client count, the more you win, is not the case. Two events a year that change a life is more profitable than 30 events a year that are cookie cutter.

Be the change.

It is important that you understand that *you* hold your future and your future decisions. You are not pigeon-holed as a planner, because planners carry a multitude of abilities to navigate special occasions and life events. Trust me; I speak from experience. Once upon a time, and even today, I knew that I must believe in my unique abilities whatever I did. Every day I had to prove I was worthy of being a planner just to stand apart from the newcomers.

Complaining takes away a part of my future, and proclaiming helps me take ahold of the unknown. Nothing is solidified but my plans, which I choose to attach to my life or someone else's. Events are every moment, every time and everywhere. Just keep that in mind. I have been an event planner for over twenty years — I am branded as a planner.

I once worked with a seasoned planner who carried creativity to the extreme. She was employed with a major corporation for over nineteen years. The year before retirement, she was laid off. Persevering, she took her skills and made a very successful event-planning firm. I was impressed by her business cards and website. She had connections and knew how to sell herself. Most importantly, she kept pictures of everyone she encountered. The event planning community knew her by first name. Her connection with her clients and planning ability set her apart from the rest. Do the same.

I believe that we were placed on this earth to leave a mark. Planners would not look as deep into this career field as I do; however, I found a meaning to my career, which makes me a history maker. I believe that we carry a power that is greater than anything in us or around us.

Hurricanes are part of Virginia's culture. With its surroundings being the Atlantic Ocean, it is common for a tropical storm to develop and touch land. During hurricane Isabel, the newscasters did whatever possible to alert viewers of potential harm. During an alert segment a newscaster viewed its networking station as a big party. You attend a party to seek an important message. I was intrigued by the newscaster's analogy.

During your pivotal event, what is your message? My message is Events carry Power.

Explain your event planning journey.

Pop Quiz

How do you create a life that is meant for you?

Whom do you trust to plan a life that is meant for you?

When is your next BREATHE?

Name a unique environmental change.

Did you start your impact-kudos journal?

Lightning Source UK Ltd.
Milton Keynes UK
UKHW021503041218
333445UK00009B/103/P